MAN IN THE

(REARVIEW)

MIR-ROR

That Time I Left Corporate America,
Became an Uber Driver, and Lived to Write About It

LARUE COOK

woodhall press
NORWALK, CT

Woodhall Press, 81 Old Saugatuck Road, Norwalk, CT 06855
Woodhallpress.com
Distributed by INGRAM

Author photo by Dan Wonderly at WonderlyImaging.com

Library of Congress Cataloging-in-Publication Data available
ISBN 978-1-949116-02-1 (paperback)
ISBN 978-1-949116-03-8 (ebook)

First Edition

In memory of my father

In every child who is born, under no matter what circumstances, and of no matter what parents, the potentiality of the human race is born again: and in [that child], too, once more, and of each of us, our terrific responsibility towards human life; towards the utmost idea of goodness, of the horror of error, and of God.

—JAMES AGEE, *Let Us Now Praise Famous Men*, 1941

We cannot escape our origins, however hard we try, those origins which contain the key—could we but find it—to all that we later become.

—JAMES BALDWIN, *Notes of a Native Son*, 1955

CONTENTS

AUTHOR'S NOTE

This is a work of creative nonfiction. Most of the events that inspired the essays in this book took place between January 2016 and August 2018. I did not use a recording device with my passengers, meaning each account is based entirely on my memory or notes taken after our trip. Passengers' names have also been changed or omitted. I was and remain an independent contractor—not an employee—for Uber and Lyft. The views expressed within are my own and do not represent those of any company or institution with which I have been or am currently affiliated.

Why the Hell I Did It

Truth is, I didn't set out in life to write a book. I grew up in Kingston, Tennessee, a small town just west of Knoxville, and spent four years at the University of Tennessee earning a degree in journalism, following in the footsteps of my late father, LaRue "Boots" Cook. He got his start as a sports writer and editor for the *Kingston Banner* in the 1950s, quickly rising to managing editor and part-owner of what would become the *Roane County News*. His sports column "What's Cooking?" turned him into a local celebrity. I came by storytelling honest, I guess, and then I was formally trained to conduct interviews and taught the importance of multiple sources, as well as the importance of putting the most pertinent facts at the beginning. "Don't bury the lede!" my professors would remind me. But perhaps nothing was more ingrained in me than objectivity, remaining on the periphery, allowing myself the distance necessary to see the story from as many angles as possible. So this exercise, putting myself directly in front of the camera, remains a bit of a foreign concept.

MAN IN THE (REARVIEW) MIRROR

I have written several drafts of this prologue, and after each one that I didn't even bother to save, I've returned to the words of essayists I admire—legends like James Baldwin, James Agee, and Joan Didion. But there is one preface in particular that continues to resonate: the 1982 introduction to E. B. White's *One Man's Meat*, written after he abruptly exited New York City (and his gig at *The New Yorker*) and moved with his wife and son to a farmhouse in Maine.

"My decision to pull up stakes was impulsive and irresponsible," he writes with the luxury of nearly half a century of hindsight. He goes on to say that he wasn't disenchanted with New York—he loved New York, as the T-shirt says—or with *The New Yorker*, or with his wife and son. "If I was disenchanted at all," he writes, "I was probably disenchanted with *me*."

I will posit in the pages to come about the reasons that prompted what I endearingly refer to as my Existential Crisis, the year I put in my two weeks' notice as a senior editor at *ESPN The Magazine*, sold my condo in Hartford, Connecticut, and moved back to Knoxville, Tennessee; the year I flew to Ireland and to Italy, my first trips outside the United States; the year I hiked in the Grand Canyon and drove the Pacific Coast Highway; the year I made less than fifteen thousand dollars on 1,716 Uber rides; the year I built a website and started sharing my life on social media. But, like E. B. White, I don't have any epiphanic moments, no cinematic scenes that led to my calculated dumb decision to leave a nearly six-figure salary and a free gym behind.

As James Baldwin writes in his 1984 preface to *Notes of a Native Son*: "I find it hard to re-create the journey. It has something to do, certainly, with what I was trying to discover and, also, trying to avoid."

If there is a tangible start date to my Existential Crisis, it is April 21, 2016, the day before I turned thirty-one and the day I found out my first published short story, "The Devil You Know," was out in *Minetta Review*, the undergrad literary journal at NYU. That was also the day I officially (finally?) joined Facebook and became an active member of Instagram, things I'd promised myself I would do if I ever became a published writer of fiction. That same night, on a whim, I posted my first #ubernights on social media, a couple of innocuous encounters with drunken college kids below Instagram-filtered photos of downtown Knoxville.

I was the rare pre-smartphone millennial who hadn't bothered to put his life or his random thoughts on the internet. Mostly because I wasn't proud of the man I'd become, far short of the man I'd promised my father I would be, standing over his comatose body at fifteen years old. I wasn't proud of my infidelities, the lying I'd been doing to others and to myself; nor was I proud of the fact that I was wallowing in unhappiness, too overcome with self-pity and self-doubt to take the first step toward finding purpose in this existence. I didn't have children or a partner, didn't own a dog or a cat, so I realized that rather than projecting a positive, albeit false narrative about my personal life, social media would be the space where I would hold myself accountable, the mirror I'd refused to look into.

This began as an unscientific social experiment, really, a way for me to reconnect with a digital world that I had been hiding from, as well as a real world that seemed to have spun out of my reach. My heart needed a jump start, and in my experience, the only way to jump-start a heart is to use people as cables, people out here just living, some of them succeeding and some of them getting by the best they can. Sometimes you feed off them; sometimes they feed off you. Sometimes being the jumper cable is the jolt, revving your own engine, reminded of the life that has lain dormant inside you.

Most nights, after I've finished my Uber/Lyft shift, I sit at my dining room table and type on my laptop between sips of beer. I write until that bottle is empty and there are a few paragraphs in front of me. I pry the cap off another bottle of beer, I read the sentences I've strung together, and I admit to myself that they aren't worth a damn, much less anyone's time. What a person does next, I've learned, is what separates writers from people who just like to drink beer.

On those nights when I sit frustrated, I go to my book shelf for the collected stories and essays of the late Raymond Carver. Admittedly, my muse, at least for a thirty-something cisgender, heterosexual white man who likes to drink beer, is rather predictable. I don't feel the need to defend my choice, though, other than to say that I don't believe Carver truly thought himself a writer until one day he woke up and he was one. He'd been published, and critics were singing his praises. Carver was living, sometimes poorly, a life about as mundane and confounding as a white man who is a tick below middle class could hope for. In his essay "On Writing," he explains that his decision to exclusively write short stories wasn't necessarily conscious, just that his attention span "had gone out" on him, that he couldn't bring himself to concentrate on reading a novel anymore, much less write one. Carver says this happened in his late twenties, around the same time he lost "any great ambitions." Then he goes on to quote the late Danish author Karen Blixen (pen name Isak Dinesen), who said that she wrote a little every day, without hope and without despair. Carver says that someday he'll write that on a three-by-five card and tape it to the wall beside his desk.

To all of that, I can relate. I haven't given up on dreaming, or believing, nor is that what Carver seems to be getting at. But there comes a moment in life when the world is a tad clearer, like when I was fifteen and put on a pair of prescription glasses for the first time, shocked at what I didn't know I was missing, how green the leaves can be in springtime. What becomes clearer is that living as honest as one can is the accomplishment, and whatever notoriety or money you get out of tinkering on a page, well, that's more than most will ever see.

After reading my essay "An Ode to Alcohol," which appears later in this collection, a close friend texted and asked, among other things, if that would be the final essay on my website. He'd sensed the longing and regret for a past that I can't return to, but one I now have the hindsight to grapple with, to comprehend how my actions have reverberated into the present and have inevitably altered my future, and the future of others. I told him that I didn't plan to ever stop writing again, and not too many days since April 21, 2016, have passed without me at least jotting something down, whether on my smartphone or my laptop or an actual piece of pulpwood. As of this writing, I'm inching toward four thousand total trips as a driver for Uber and Lyft. I've been driving people around for their stories, and in the process, I've found mine. ◆

The Day
My Father Died

On December 10, 2000, my father quit breathing. I was fifteen. He was seventy-four. You did read that right, and I was his biological son, born to a mother thirty years his junior—his second wife, and we were his second life. I was an uncle the minute I entered the world, with a brother and a sister more than twice my age. The Cook family patriarch died on a Sunday, sometime in the morning. The sun was up, but it was overcast and cold, at least cold for Kingston, Tennessee.

My father died at home in the spare room where we'd set up his bed for hospice care. He'd been living on a ventilator at the hospital for a week, ever since he stumbled off a sidewalk and smacked his head on the concrete after leaving my high school basketball game in a nearby town. His brain had hemorrhaged profusely because of the blood thinner he took to keep a clot from hitting his mechanical valve. With your ear up to his chest, you could hear his heart *click* . . . *click* . . . *click*. But my family eventually agreed to pull the plug, and the valve marked time for two more nights.

I grew up in a modest house, one story, about thirteen hundred square feet. It was smaller when my father bought the two-bedroom in the 1950s, back before I was even a thought, back when what would one day become my bedroom was a one-car garage. The spare room where he died was also where we kept our first and only computer, a makeshift office for my father, who was retired but still worked as a local radio personality and as a PR man for a nearby school district, writing human interest stories that appeared in the county newspaper. He'd actually been the sports editor and an advertising salesman—before becoming managing editor and part-owner—of that paper the same decade he'd purchased the house, back when a man without a college degree and no formal training could do such a thing.

That was the only house I'd known, red brick with white vinyl siding trim, atop a steep hill that had a weeping willow tree in the middle of it. The tree was magical to me, like something out of a children's book, enormous and neon green, its branches drooping from the mossy weight. My father would rock with me in our white front porch swing and sing an old folk song, "Bury Me Beneath the Weeping Willow." We couldn't see them beneath the soil, but the willow's roots were as vast as its branches and had begun to wrap around the town's water lines. So the city cut the willow down when I was a little boy, and I cried. That was the first time I experienced what it is to lose a part of yourself—no consolation, no regeneration, just a gaping hole in your universe.

I'm writing this at thirty-one years old, the night before the sixteenth anniversary of my father's death. I've been on this earth now longer without my father than with him. I've written several thousand words, trying to recount the final days of his life through my fifteen-year-old eyes, but I've deleted most of them. I will write them some-day, but I might need sixteen more years before I can do my fifteen-year-old self justice. I can't explain the chasm that opens after a loss like that, a chasm between who I might've been and who I became. I can't make sense for you how I was able to start stitching up my heart the minute it'd been broken, to be so stoic, to not miss a day of school or a basketball practice while my mother helped bathe my father with a sponge and slept in a recliner next to him in the ICU.

I can't fathom how on the same day I watched my father be low-ered into the ground I also took a chemistry final in a classroom by myself, just me and the teacher, who'd allowed me to finish it during lunch. I made an A, by a point. I don't have it in me, not in the wee hours of this morning, to describe the antiseptic ER room, or the slack-jawed expression on my father's blank face as I stood over him prior to his brain surgery. I could comprehend, even at that age, that his spirit was already lifted, that the angels had already taken their share.

I felt the need to write this simply as proof of the thing occur-ring. I felt the need to own the walling off I've done, the cliché coping mechanism I've created, the digging of a hole without knowing the shovel was in my hands. I miss my father. I do. But he exists, for now, in a place I can't exorcise, any more than I can replicate the carefree smile of that blond-headed fifteen-year-old, the light in his blue eyes.

A few weeks ago, I picked up a Catholic priest on a Sunday night, his clergy collar still neat and tight. He was taking an Uber to down-town Knoxville for a beer with friends after giving his sermons and making his rounds. I told him I'd been raised Lutheran in a town run by Baptists. He smiled at that. I said I'd rarely missed a Sunday until I went to college, but that I can count on two hands the times I've been back in the pew since. "The Lord and I are still on speaking terms, though," I said. He gently laughed at that, and then shifted to the subject of my day job.

"I write fiction," I said. "I write a lot about characters who struggle with free will and blind faith, why it is people do the awful things that they do, and then spend their lives searching for an answer."

The priest was quiet for a while, considering my insinuation that free will and blind faith are mutually exclusive. "Free will is God's greatest gift," he said. "Because without it, there is really no true love of God." The priest told me of St. Bernard of Clairvaux, a French abbot who wrote a book that dissects the stages of human love for the Christian God. The priest said I should read it, if for nothing more than fodder for stories. But I figure a priest doesn't ever stop being a fisher of men, does he?

Never one to dismiss honest advice, I read passages from Clairvaux and the stages begin out of selfish love, out of love equated to the literal hunger for a mother's milk, a love for the one who assuages hunger. Then comes the love of an earthly father, a love of free will, a love of a person that is a choice. I hadn't considered it, but my father was my friend, a man I didn't need to survive, but one I wanted to be a part of my survival. My brother and sister had grown old enough to have a relationship with our father as adults, and while I don't talk to them much about his death, I'd say they have regrets, things they would've said had they known a Friday night in December would suddenly be the last time they'd hear his voice. I do not feel regret because I was with him right up until the end, nothing left unsaid, no apologies necessary because I had yet to accumulate the mistakes that would later come.

MAN IN THE (REARVIEW) MIRROR

Regret, I believe, is an adult emotion, one that you can only experience once you've put enough life behind you to appreciate never being able to live it over. If there is any regret or sadness to be found in my father's death, it is in the fact that I let his death teach me to shut out the world. And that has caused more regret and more sadness than any death, because I've spent my adult life avoiding the potential pain that comes with loving someone more than yourself.

In the scheme of existence, human life is fleeting. That is an unequivocal fact. But when you are faced with life's tangibleness at such an early yet formative age, as I was, you reexamine your own shelf life. You reexamine the human need for love, which can bring pain. You reexamine the need to breed new life, which can bring pain. You reexamine your very existence, which is only an earthly endeavor, one that you've now seen come and you've seen go, one that you have seen be relatively erased with the passage of time. You begin to seriously believe that love isn't worth the return on investment.

That's why this is an apology, not a tribute—an apology to my mother, first and foremost, for distancing myself from the woman who raised me, the only woman who has loved me unconditionally. But an apology also to the women who've had to suffer through, hoping they would see that carefree smile or the light in my eyes again, only to be disappointed. I've hurt them in ways that I will explain. I just don't have the space or context to do those women justice here, other than to say that I was unfairly asking them to carry a cross that wasn't theirs to bear. On each anniversary of my father's death, since leaving that redbrick house on that steep hill in Kingston, Tennessee, I've considered the collateral damage I've created, and I can finally acknowledge that the war has never been between anyone other than myself and God, the only one I can blame for taking my father, my only true love. ◆

Eugene's Mother

I had no expectations when I signed up to be an Uber driver in Hartford, Connecticut, and then in Knoxville, Tennessee, returning to my home state after nearly eight years. I'd walked out on my job as a senior editor for ESPN at thirty years old with enough money saved to just drive people around when I got bored. I hadn't helped anyone but myself in longer than I care to admit. I'd gotten caught up in "white privilege" problems, or "white male" problems, or whatever qualifier you want to use to say that I'd quit appreciating my circumstances, started creating perceived chips on my shoulder to justify my own unhappiness, frustrated with how simple and unsatisfying it'd been to go from lower middle-class to a tad better than white America's above-average norm.

And that's the beauty of Uber, at least for me: to discover society outside the corporate bubble, to see "Eugene" on one end, and he sees my cheesy grin on the other—two people who would've otherwise never met, never found any shared experience. Modern day

11

hitchhiking, only I wasn't planning for Eugene to have his mother with him too, and Mother had a cane and sat up front with me. She could hardly see over the dash.

"We're headed to the credit union," Eugene said from the backseat. "Then on to get something to eat, if that's alright."

Eugene's mother piped up: "I reckon this is the last time I'll be gettin' into town for a while. Surgery coming up. Doctor has to straighten out my intestines, found a blind loop of all things. Liquid diet starting soon, my last supper, I guess you'd say."

She craned back to look at her son, affirming with a "Right, Eugene?"

He said that it was. Although the young man's real name wasn't Eugene, his was a name that Southerners tend to draw out on the first syllable, elongate the vowels until it sounds more phonetically like, "You-gene." I told Eugene's mother that I hoped the surgery helped right the pain, also falling into the cadences and diction of my upbringing, the place where "fixin' to" doesn't have anything to do with repairing what's broken.

"I've worked awful hard most of my life," she said, "and it's caught up to me."

"Heavy liftin'," I said.

"Oldest of five—helped Momma carry the little ones, movin' furniture outside to sun. We'd help Granddaddy harvest tobacco and sack his potatoes—fifty-pound bags."

"Tobacco farming ain't easy."

"No, it ain't, slingin' them stalks up in the barn to cure. My hands would be black as coal when we'd tie it off into bundles."

"Makes your lungs look the same," I said and let out a nervous laugh, like you do when the truth of what you've said hits too hard.

"I've been smoking since I's seventeen."

"Hard to keep from it back then," I said.

"You'd get a high from just walking in the barn. It'd be December 'fore the leaves were dry—smelled awful good, though, like Christmas money." She craned her neck and grinned.

Eugene's mother wore thick glasses, and so did Eugene. In fact, Eugene might as well have been his mother: dark-headed, eyes as round as an owl's, with about as much of a neck, only Eugene didn't have a hump in his back. I figured Eugene's mother suffered from osteoporosis, like my grandmother, not enough calcium in their bones, common in women of their generation. My grandmother didn't harvest tobacco, though. Her backbreaking was done in the sewing room of a hosiery mill.

We arrived at the local credit union, and Eugene asked if I'd pull up far enough so he could use the drive-thru, the one where you stick your deposit in a capsule and it's shot through a pipe over to the cashier at the window. I could tell Eugene was a tad younger than me, and I wondered if his attachment to his mother had held him behind the times.

"Sure do make cars boxy these days," Eugene's mother said, commenting on my Honda Civic. "They don't make 'em like Chevelles anymore. My husband's been dead eleven years. We used to love antique car shows, before Eugene came along."

I told her that my father had me late in life, that he always preferred a Buick or a Pontiac.

"Smart," she said. "American-made."

My phone pinged. Eugene had entered the second destination: Austin's Steakhouse and Homestyle Buffet. Eugene must've felt left out of the conversation, because he started going on about some new navigation app that alerts you to where police are sitting and traffic jams, rerouting you in real time. Eugene said that users could even put in suggested routes, letting people know which way they think is faster, how to miss a stoplight or two. Eugene's mother and I listened, but we didn't have much to offer, although I was a bit confused about Eugene's interest in navigation when he was the one calling me for a ride. Maybe Eugene just needed a way to pass the time, same as anybody.

As we rolled into the parking lot of the steakhouse, I told Eugene's mother that I'd be thinking of her, the surgery, fixing the blind loop.

"Lord willing, I'll be in my flower garden by July," she said.

It was late May. I glanced at her cane and remembered how she'd barely made it down her front steps, wouldn't have without Eugene's extended arm. I wondered if Eugene was staying in the nest because of his mother, or if he simply didn't have any other prospects. I nodded to them as Eugene helped his mother climb out.

"You have a good one, sweetheart," Eugene's mother said.

I idled at the front door of Austin's Steakhouse and Homestyle Buffet and considered how genuine Eugene's mother had been, how in a former life that would've pained me, for happiness to come so easy at an all-you-can-eat steakhouse. Nowadays, I wish "sweetheart" from Eugene's mother was enough happiness to get me to tomorrow. ◆

Kumar's Mother

As Uber has increased in popularity, more and more people have started calling in rides for someone else, a family member or significant other. So you can imagine the confusion that can arise when I arrive to pick up a person based on name alone, as was the case when I showed up to get "Kumar" at an assisted-living facility on the outskirts of downtown Knoxville. Instead, out walked a tiny, bespectacled woman wearing a sari. I assumed she was kin to Kumar and didn't ask any questions, but she continued to question how it was that I knew her son.

"Work friend? You go to school with my grandson?" she asked, still hesitant to climb in my backseat.

I explained that Kumar was paying me to drive her home, to an affluent suburb about half an hour away. She opened the back door and situated herself.

"This no cab," she said.

I did my best to relate the concept of Uber, although I saw Kumar's mother in the rearview simply cock her head to one side, same as my own grandmother does when I talk about what I'm doing for a living these days. But Kumar's mother seemed to be more relaxed now, and I kept on with the icebreaking: "Visiting family?"

"My husband," she said. "Stroke, months ago. We could not make trip to Holy Temple for first time in very long time." She sighed. I glanced back to see her bunching up her sari, rubbing it between her hands.

"Do you know India?" she asked. I said I'd never been, but that I had fallen hard for Mira Nair's Punjabi comedy, *Monsoon Wedding*, while earning my minor in cinema—the intricate color schemes of the ceremony, the pomp and circumstance of the preparation, all reminds us that our customs, albeit oceans apart, connect us more than we'd care to admit.

"Yes, yes. Hindu, like that," she said. "God is good—I have prayed every day and visiting my husband every day. He walks again, saying some words. The doctors said he would do nothing." I told Kumar's mother that I hoped her husband would be well enough to reach India again. "God will make it so," she said.

As the conversation had its twists and turns, she and I learned that we'd both lived in New York City, and we fondly recalled our time there, hers spent on the Upper West Side, running a printing company with her husband. Mine was spent in Queens, between Sunnyside and Jackson Heights, the latter just off the Roosevelt Avenue stop, where she agreed you can find some of the best Indian food this side of Delhi. A couple of years ago, Kumar's mother and her husband retired and, as is the custom, moved south to be with Kumar and his two sons.

"Do you have wife and children?" she asked. I considered deflecting with an old adage or cliché, but there's something to be said for language barriers, having to relate in the simplest of terms: "One day, God willing," I said.

When we arrived at the destination, Kumar's mother said that she received a text saying her son had been delayed at work, wires had crossed within the family, and that had been the reason for her first Uber ride. "You are a good man," she said. "I will pray for God to bless you."

I could not think of a more adequate reply than "Thank you."

Probably about the time Kumar's mother walked through the front door, I saw a text drop down from the top of my phone screen. It was from Kumar: "God will bless you." Driving to look for my next passenger, I couldn't help but think of my own grandmother, a good Christian woman, who overcame poverty and an eighth-grade education and a first husband with a wandering eye, not to mention breast cancer, to reach eighty-two and counting and to have a front porch overlooking the lake, where she can rock in her rocker and drink coffee and enjoy her three great-grandchildren thanks to my two cousins.

"The Lord sure has been good to me," she has said many, many times before, the steam rising from her coffee on a cool Sunday morning. I imagine she and Kumar's mother would have some stories to tell each other, once they could begin to understand each other's accents and vernaculars. As for myself, I'd be pulling one over on you if I didn't admit that since my father fell and smacked his head on the concrete when I was fifteen, I've spent many nights wondering if anyone's on the other end, wondering if it's even worth praying anymore.

But there in that empty car, the headlights the only light on the road, I whispered, "Can't you just let 'em both be right?" to anyone who'd listen. ◆

The Man Who
Needed a Lift

Every now and again, I take a break from Ubering college kids around Knoxville and head to Nashville to drive tourists and bachelorette parties around Music City. I justify the trip because I get to visit family and an old college friend, hit a honky-tonk or two, live up to the stereotype of what it is to be Southern. That's what had me down in Nashville over Memorial Day weekend. It was a Sunday, tourists and locals still drinking heavy, with Monday off to nurse hangovers and catch flights.

Around noon, I got a call to the outskirts of downtown, where the cranes of gentrification had only begun to build the high-rises necessary to accommodate white flight into derelict neighborhoods. The apartment complex I pulled up to was nice enough—a few stories, new-looking with a generic deli on the bottom floor. A man who appeared to be in his early thirties, about my age, came out of a side exit wearing a Misfits T-shirt, khaki shorts, and flip-flops with white crew-cut socks. His tan was thick but not in any ethnic way, probably from roofing or construction, something that would keep a white man out in the sun against his wishes.

"Can you take me to a gas station?" he said as he climbed in the passenger seat.

"Sure, which one?" I asked. I didn't want to let on that I was out of my main territory and not too familiar with this part of town.

"One of the Indian ones—dot not feather—that sells bongs and shit," he said. He laughed, and I noticed he was missing some teeth in the back and had several silver caps. He had a five o'clock shadow already.

"I can find one on the GPS," I said.

"Naw," he said, "just take a right here, go toward the hood. One on every other corner."

"What kind of cigarettes you looking for?" I asked.

"I ain't lookin' for no cigarettes," he said. "I'm lookin' for some get-it-up pills. All the Indian stores have 'em. Me and my buddy got two girls comin' over, and I can't have any 'failures to launch.'" He actually did air quotes. "Know what I mean?" He quickly pointed to a run-down Phillips 66 that no longer sold gas but still had pumps out front and plenty of beer signs in the windows. "Perfectoooo," he yelled.

I stopped and he was back out in under five minutes, opening the door with a grin. "Perfectoooo," he yelled again. "Indian guy says one of these will have me going seven hours straight." He immediately ripped open the box of pills and read the directions aloud: "Take one pill with warm water that has been boiled." He looked at me incredulously. "How's my wiener gonna know if I boiled the water first?" I forced a laugh because this was kind of funny and because I wasn't sure what else to do.

"Can you take me to that minimart we passed back aways?" he asked. "I'm hungry now." En route, he read the ingredients: "Sea Horse?" He nudged my shoulder. "Really, sea horse helps?" I forced another laugh. "Penis Ettestis, Something or Other, Yak Testis . . . YAK TESTIS? Well, kin to a bull, right?" he said. "What a man will put in his body to get it up." He shook his head, eyes still on the ingredients. I shrugged a shrug that said I was completely at a loss about whether to go genuine or sarcastic on impotency.

"My buddy and me been drinkin' since Friday night," he said, "and there's just nothin' down there—put on some pornography and everything. Still nothing." I nodded, without laughing, as we pulled into the minimart. He was in and out with a bag of Starburst jelly beans.

"Alllrrrriiiight," he said. "Ready for some lovin'." He rubbed his hands together furiously. "So, where ya from?" he asked.

"Small town outside Knoxville," I said.

"What's it called?" he asked, ripping open the jelly beans.

"Kingston," I said.

He slapped the dash while chomping on a mouthful of jelly beans. "No fuckin' way. You know Cedar Grove Baptist?"

I did. I said that I went to vacation bible school there once.

"Went to that church till I's five," he said, "till Momma moved us. You know the woman they called Dot and her husband, Red?"

I said that I'd heard of ol' Red and Dot.

He wheezed a throat-clearing laugh through the jelly beans. "Yep. Ol' Red and Dot. Them was my grandparents."

"Get back to Kingston much?" I asked.

He took a beat and chomped and stared out over the road, tilting his head and wincing, like maybe he was waiting for a sharp pain to pass. "Long way from Kingston these days."

We returned to the complex where I picked him up. "Well, small world," I said.

He tore off a couple of "get-it-up" pills from the sleeve and stretched them out to me. "Here, these'll make it bigger." He wheezed that laugh, and I was too appreciative of the joke not to take them. I forced one last laugh. I couldn't help but wonder why he'd veered off one way and I'd headed the other, two good ol' boys from Kingston, raised in a house of the Lord.

"Best of luck to ya, brother," he said and waved, downing the bag of Starburst jelly beans as he walked away. ◆

Man in the (Rearview) Mirror

PART 1

A friend and a reader of my website asked me a question recently that I haven't been able to shake: "Where are *you* in all of these essays? Isn't this your Existential Crisis?" Sure, I am *there*, moving the plot along with an aphorism or smart-aleck one-liner, stepping back to offer perspective for where it is I'm writing from, occasionally giving a glimpse of what's rolling around in my head. My friend is right, though. I've protected myself with varying degrees of separation from you, the reader, and from the people who pay me to drive them around. I've been more journalist than essayist, more camera lens than mirror.

The view from my rearview is inherently tinted, perhaps even clouded by my current station in life, by the time and the place I find myself in. And while that might sound like an abstract notion, I don't believe that it is. The time and place I find myself in is quite concrete: I'm back at the beginning, back in Knoxville, Tennessee, the town where I graduated from college nearly a decade ago, back at the precipice of this existential journey—despite my insistence that it's only just begun. It was along these streets, within these academic halls, at the counters and on the patios of these bars and restaurants and concert venues that bear different names and new facades, that I discovered this intangible need to express myself within the infinite space that lies between the period and the next capital letter.

But then, somewhere between Knoxville and the East River and Mark Twain's house, I lost the meaning between the lines, lost sight of the complexity that exists within the simple telling of our stories. Maybe that's why I'm back here, where the words used to connect, where the sentences made sense. Or maybe I'm back in the place where the words were safe from scrutiny, not burdened with the weight of livelihood or merit or someone else's expectations. These are the thoughts that punctuate my trips, that fill the void from one passenger to the next. I get paid, sure, but I'd be lying if I said the stories of others aren't my lifeblood. I suck everything out of them I can, coax every detail, praying that within their lines I'll find my point again—or at least take my mind off the fact that I'm not certain I have one left in me.

Contrary to the previous scenes I've painted, my nights aren't all that colorful. I spend several hours in my car alone. Unlike major metropolitan cities, the non-college citizens of Knoxville haven't completely warmed up to Uber yet. So if I want to fund this Existential Crisis, I must drive the drunk shifts, which usually consist of shuttling twenty-somethings from the hot spots around campus and downtown directly back to the very row of apartment complexes where they will request me to pick them up the following night. There ain't much substance is what I'm saying, although there is the occasional sign of life.

Like Jun, an exchange student from Shanghai I met this week, and who is researching the densest stars in our galaxy, studying their molecular makeup, attempting to unlock their mysteries. Or Chad, a doctoral candidate in astronomy, who left behind life as a rock 'n' roll drummer to focus on the Kuiper belt, orbiting out there somewhere beyond Neptune and home to Pluto, which I'll always think of as a planet with a chip on its shoulder. Or the three thirty-something white women who pleaded for me to stop at a fast-food restaurant after their "buck wild" weeknight and continued to remind me that they weren't apologizing for the amount of calories in the grease-bottomed bags I handed over, even though I'd offered no judgment to begin with. Or the six-foot-three, 280-pound (his measurements) black man whose Uber handle is "Big Papa" and who's been a bouncer around Knoxville for years, and who admitted that he'd rather not have a career predicated on his fists and stature and skin color. He told me this after I listened to him expertly negotiate the dismissal of a "booty call" (his words) to instead enjoy a footlong sub and cream stout and a night on the couch.

I could spin a yarn out of any of those, stretch them to effect, whether that be humor or poignancy or perhaps even genius, because I'm a firm believer that genius can be found in every encounter of our lives, if we put the brakes on long enough to see it. Of course, I was a journalist, and while there is innate ability required, I did go to school for four years to learn how to figuratively and literally read people, to become a chameleon, to extract their stories and assume their emotions, often without their being the wiser. I spent last week's Uber nights considering my friend's question, the meaningfulness that I've been imposing on the moments of others, the fairness of that, the self-gratification in dissecting others' insecurities while ignoring my own.

It was on my mind Tuesday night when I scooped up a trio of college kids who'd left a concert early, once the opener went off-stage. I inquired about an opener worth the price of admission, and the guy up front said, "These new kids called Bear Hands." I did a double take. Bear Hands are not "new" or "kids." They are an indie rock (whatever that means anymore) quartet I first saw on the Lower East Side in 2007, my first winter living in Queens and working in Manhattan as an intern for *Entertainment Weekly*. I immediately scrolled through Spotify for that long-lost EP, wanting these kids to understand that whatever they heard in that brand-spanking-new concert venue had evolved from what I'd heard in a tiny bar called Pianos a lifetime ago, when I thought I could waltz into the Big Apple and write about music and movies and pop culture, just like every other kid—although every other kid had graduated from an expensive college that had a journalism school with a proper name attached to it.

If you've ever fancied yourself an audiophile, Bear Hands was, for me, that "I saw them when" band, a group you thought was surely going to be a headliner sooner than later. My first byline in a national magazine (all sixty-five words) was a review of their first EP, *Golden*. Then three years disappeared before their first album was released, by which time I'd mostly traded writing for a full-time editing gig at ESPN. The indie rock scene had also evolved from old-fashioned guitar shredding and hi-hatting and a heavy dose of kick drum to synths and keyboards and overproduced samples, and their debut went mostly unnoticed.

I put *Golden* on repeat the rest of the night, trying to convince passengers leaving the show that this was the same group they'd watched open for Silversun Pickups, a band that also had its seminal indie moment around the time I arrived in NYC, one that fell relatively by the wayside for similar reasons. The rhythm and the beat of *Golden* had lost its luster, as tends to happen as tastes mature. But I was keenly aware that the lyrics of the young Bear Hands were empty to me now, perhaps always had been. The words rang well next to one another, yet when examined, were mostly hollow.

So I cued up the single that had them back in rotation, "2AM," a song that features a keyboard and the slightest of synths and is about dealing with all your friends being sober and going out being a drag and all your favorite spots being closed and making love being "fine," but really just wanting to forget how old you are. Most of the people I gave rides to were around my age, and that song had resonated with them, although I'm not sure why it had with those college kids earlier, other than maybe their having some confused idea that growing up occurs from eighteen to twenty-two. The older riders and I, we reminisced about where we were when we first heard this band and that band, how we mark our lives with music and the bars we were in and the company we kept in that time and that place, how a part of us will always remain there, in that haze of unadulterated happiness.

I actually interviewed Bear Hands once for a profile that ran in the *New York Press*, a now-defunct alt-weekly, a sad truth which seems to be a recurring fate for the places I've been published—save for "The Worldwide Leader in Sports." The four guys were simply glad to be asked questions, glad to have been compensated in what amounted to beer money for doing what they loved. The same could be said for me then. Driving to and from that venue on Tuesday night, picking up patrons and concert promoters and even a rep for a major record label, I thought about what I would ask those men nine years later, wondered if they envisioned themselves still play-ing opener in a college town for a band whose most-popular single on Spotify is from 2006. I wanted to ask them if they lost a piece of themselves in the process, if they would transport back to that night at Pianos on the Lower East Side if they could and reverse course, knowing what they know now, maybe dig their heels in a bit deeper, or maybe just walk.

I'd like to think they'd say they're content to still be penning lines, still drawing crowds, however small, to hear their chords. I'd like to think they'd say whatever part of them was lost has been regained, albeit at an inevitable cost, the same cost any of us must suffer in any profession, in any station in life. I'd like to think they'd say they put on *Golden*, too, every once in a while, and that they're nostalgic, painfully nostalgic, but also at peace with leaving that part of themselves in that time and in that place, that whatever "sell-ing out" they might've done, pandering to record labels or agents or audiences, was a necessary rite of passage. I'd like to think they'd say the reward is to still be musicians, getting slightly more than beer money, although their taste in beer probably ain't as cheap. ◆

Things About Me You Oughta Know

I

I've been thinking an awful lot about the word *change*. There's no denying that I'd arrived at a point in my life when I needed one—up and leaving ESPN and returning to Tennessee was about the only way I was going to become whole again. The word stayed on my mind often this past Fourth of July weekend, as my mother turned sixty and the United States turned 240, as we celebrated our independence, our freedom, maybe even forgot for more than a few beers the predicament our nation finds itself in, forgot all about Hillary Rodham and Donald J. and everything else up for debate. I'm nearing 750 Uber trips—from Connecticut to Tennessee—and I believe I've talked to enough people, canvassed enough generations to tell you that this is one of the most monumental periods in America's relatively short history.

It seems like a lifetime ago that Barack Obama told us our country could use a *change*, doesn't it? In the spirit of this Existential Crisis, and in the spirit of this relationship between you and me, there is something you oughta know: I did not cast a ballot in that historic 2008 election when Barack Obama became our first black president. Something else you oughta know about me is that I'm a white boy who is obsessed with hip-hop, have been since I snuck home a friend's copy of Tupac's *Greatest Hits* on CD when I was in the eighth grade. I've become a student of the genre, following it from subculture to its pinnacle as pop culture, and I have a particular affinity for a talented young rapper named Vince Staples, whom I saw live at the fifteenth anniversary of the Bonnaroo music festival. When I'm on Uber rides with college-age kids, I'll sneak in a track or two of Vince's—in between Drake and Future—and while I'm not saying that his debut LP, *Summertime '06*, is for everyone, I'd ask you to indulge me by considering these lines from his song "Norf Norf," a sort of Sam Cooke send up, albeit less hopeful: *School wasn't no fun, couldn't bring my gun/Knowin' change gone come like Obama and them say/But they shootin' everyday round my mama and them way/So we put an AK where Kiana and them stay/And that's for any n---a say he got a problem with me.*

I'm not sure when exactly Vince penned those lines, but the album they're on was released in 2015, so I imagine he wrote them at least a year before we could've foreseen a clash between The Donald and HRC; back before the massacre at a gay nightclub in Orlando; back before Brexit; back before Facebook Live was invented to capture a policeman killing Philando Castile; back before talk of building a wall; back before 2016 became a watershed year for us, although I'm starting to wonder what "us" means anymore. As Vince would probably remind me, I don't have a clue about growing up on the streets of Long Beach, wouldn't have the slightest idea what *change* might look like to him and his mama. But I do know what it is to be indifferent, fatalistic even, to balance my patriotism with a heavy dose of proverbial AK—to question just how much "they" can *change* the disconnect between "us."

For the first time in a long time, I spent the entire Fourth of July weekend in Kingston, Tennessee, with family, with the people I love, people I believe would take a bullet for me, people I believe would shoot one for me if they had to. I'd like to believe I'd do the same, if it was us or them—I'd just have to borrow one of their pistols. I sat at the dinner table and listened to some of them reminisce, as I often have, about that vague, rose-colored era before this country "went to hell in a handbasket," back before Obama had changed the fact that a black man had never been in the White House, or the fact that two men could marry.

My mother would later tell me, sitting on my screened-in front porch in Knoxville, that that's all we know, that we'd stop on the side of the road to fix a flat for any person, no matter their color, that she's seen it with her own eyes. My mother told me that we only wish everyone, whatever their creed, had to work hard for a living again, that everyone, no matter what letter of LGBTQ they fall under, had to be held accountable again, that we only wish children could pray to the Lord in schools again, that we only want to feel safe again, that we carry guns on our hips or in our boots because you never know anymore. She told me that most people ain't gonna *change*, no matter what I write; that people, in her experience, don't tend to *change* anyway. And so I asked her if she hadn't watched her son change these last six months. I asked her if I ought to just give up on this nonsense, driving people around and writing about it, if it ain't gonna change nothin' nohow.

My mother pursed her lips and was quiet for a minute. She shook her head no. She shrugged her shoulders and told me to go on and do what I'm doin', that I'm going to anyhow. My mother said, "I'll be behind you, even if people quit readin'."

Still, this past weekend, on the Fourth of July, I sat at the dinner table and did what I told myself I wouldn't. I turned my eyes down and kept on eating my ribs and coleslaw, letting apathy get the better of me, not speaking up for Obama or for the LGBTQ community. I licked my fingers and stacked up the cleaned plates and went on, without saying a thing. I went and rocked on my grandmother's front porch by myself and thought about a ride I'd had the week prior with Ms. Johnson, a black woman in her sixties whom I took to physical therapy. Ms. Johnson and her son had been in a car accident. They were at a stop sign when a flatbed truck carrying metal beams went in reverse.

"My son looked at me and said, 'Momma, he ain't stoppin','" Ms. Johnson said. "My son said, 'Momma, you gonna have to jump.'" So Ms. Johnson and her son dove out of the car, just before those metal beams smashed through the windshield. She handed her phone to me so I could see the damage in a picture.

"Why was he backing up at a stop sign?"

"Policeman asked the same thing," Ms. Johnson laughed. "I said, 'Mr. Policeman, I sure would like to know, too. Wouldn't I like to know, too.' I bet ya he was on them pills that keep a person up all hours. Lord knows them truckers are always poppin' pills, tryin' to make a paycheck, you know what I'm sayin'?" I nodded. "You don't pop them pills, do ya?"

"No, ma'am," I said, falling into my Southern call and response.

"So this all you do, drive folks here, there, and yonder?" Ms. Johnson asked.

"For the moment," I said, "until I figure out what's next. I volunteer too, just started over at the Boys & Girls Club."

Ms. Johnson said she was a volunteer herself, now that she's retired, that she even brought a few of the kids home with her when parents had to work late. "Feed 'em Kool-Aid and PB&J," Ms. Johnson said. "Keep 'em away from all the nonsense for a night. Can't tell kids nothin' today, you know what I'm sayin'?"

"They're a handful," I said, "but I can't discipline anyway, not as a volunteer."

"Wouldn't matter," Ms. Johnson said. "They wouldn't listen." We let that thought hang there. "Just like my grandson," Ms. Johnson said after a beat. I saw her shake her head slowly in the rearview. "Came walkin' up to me the other day," she said, "then I seen his momma and daddy trailin' him. I said, 'Oh, Lord, what you done now,' you know what I'm sayin'?" I nodded. "I said, 'You got a girl pregnant? You in trouble with the police?' My grandson said, 'No, ma'am. Grandmamma, I'm gonna join the army. I'm tired of these dead-end jobs.'"

"So you don't like that idea?" I asked.

Ms. Johnson shook her head some more. "I don't like it at all. Says he wants to be military police. Says he's gonna get training in another language." Ms. Johnson's voice rose an octave. "He don't have to tell me—he's talkin' 'bout that Pakistan. Just ain't safe no more."

"Not much safer here some days," I said.

"You know you right," Ms. Johnson said. "So you ain't got no wife, no kids?"

"No kids," I said.

"No woman?" Ms. Johnson pressed.

"I've had a couple of girlfriends," I said, "but they're still back where I used to be."

"They leave you, you leave them?" she asked.

"I guess I left 'em both, but I really lost 'em both," I said, giving Ms. Johnson about a fourth of the truth.

"You treat 'em wrong, son?"

"I wouldn't say I treated 'em right."

"They stay mad at ya?" Ms. Johnson asked.

"I apologized," I said. "But I'd say they might still be mad."

"And you still runnin'," Ms. Johnson said.

"I guess I'm not ready to face who I was then," I said.

"Son, even the worst of us still got some good in us," Ms. Johnson said. "You'll get right, in your own time."

"You should be proud of your grandson," I said, switching the subject. "Sounds like he just wants a better life. And he's fighting for our country." I looked up in the rearview. Ms. Johnson stared out the window, then turned her eyes to mine. She wore glasses and her cheeks were loose, her dark hair in a short perm, not too unlike my own grandmother's.

"You probably right," she said. "But I just don't see no reason, all this ISIS, all this Pakistan stuff. Let 'em in, now we can't get 'em out."

I slouched behind the wheel. I turned my eyes from hers and drove on without saying a thing, same as I did at my grandmother's dinner table on the Fourth of July.

II

On a Monday during rush hour, a few weeks before I met Ms. Johnson, I picked up a blind man. He was not the first blind man I'd given a ride to, although my only previous encounter was merely

33

a five-minute drive. That blind man spent most of the time on his phone, asking an employee at Cracker Barrel if someone would be kind enough to meet us outside to escort him to his seat in the dining area. I had so many questions then: How had he read my texts prior to the pickup? How long had he been without vision? How'd he lose his sight? But those are questions that require a certain amount of trust, a trust I must build on every trip if my passenger and I are going to have a conversation of any substance.

It's a characteristic I pride myself on, being someone people feel they can open up to, at least for the miles they're in my car. I assume the ease lies in my seeming lack of judgment, the quick admission of my own sins. And let us not ignore the mirror: I'm a baby-faced, bespectacled, fair-haired, thirty-one-year-old white man with a master's degree who drives a 2012 Honda Civic with leather interior. As society's standards go, I'm about as harmless and, dare I say, vanilla as Larry on the first season of *Orange Is the New Black*.

The blind man I picked up on that Monday, however, couldn't see any of that. He could not gauge my demeanor, could not size me up by my pigment, could not do anything other than judge me based on the sound of my Southern drawl, which is returning slightly after seven years in the Northeast. When I saw that the ride would be twelve minutes, I prepared those questions I hadn't had time to ask before, intrigued by a potential story. I already assumed this man was educated, having emerged from a children's hospital in blue scrubs and a white coat. He also appeared to be of Native American descent, his skin a dusty brown, his shoe-polish black hair knotted in a single braid that reached the middle of his back.

I'm reminded now of how heightened a person's senses can become once he or she has lost one. So I can only assume that as we were exchanging pleasantries—he'd been held up at work and was rushing home to change clothes, asking if I'd give him a lift back to town—this blind man must've felt the movement of the car, must've been able to decipher the exact turns.

"Which way are you going?" he asked with uncertainty.

My GPS had sent me to the nearby interstate to avoid traffic, but the blind man told me that I wasn't going the direction of the interstate, a hint of hurt in his voice, a hint of panic that I was taking advantage of him. I resented the insinuation, although I wonder now if his perceived slight might've simply been in what author and poet Claudia Rankine called my "white imagination" in an interview with *The Guardian*. The blind man could likely hear the indignation in my voice, and in his mind's eye, we weren't two human beings anymore but rather a man who'd lost his sight and one who had not. I asked if he'd like me to turn around, to go the way his senses were telling him. He quietly said no.

Frustrated by the idea that he might still think I was milking him for a few extra bucks, I broke the awkward silence with each direction to prove my honesty, although, with the luxury of hindsight, I realize that he might never have been able to see, that perhaps my step-by-step directions were received as condescension, that he was genuinely scared, there in his darkness.

When we pulled onto his street, the blind man finally spoke again. He told me that his house was the one with the large, second-story deck. He cracked a joke about his yard being overgrown, that mowing was atop his to-do list. I was too uncertain, too nervous that I might say something offensive, to ask if he could actually mow his own yard, if he had to walk through the grass to gauge its height against his legs.

"Do you still want me to wait?" I asked, idling on his carport.

"We're good," he said, which I took, in my insecurity, to mean that he'd had enough of me, that he would request another Uber for his next trip. So I backed out, assuming he heard me scrape the bottom of my car on the lip of his driveway. Then, not five minutes later, I received a text from the blind man, asking where I'd gone. I immediately stopped and replied that it was a miscommunication, that I would gladly pick him up if he could wait.

"No," was his reply.

I spent the rest of the day defeated, a sinking sensation in my gut. I even discussed the incident with some of my passengers, pleaded my case to people who could see. And they did side with me—sided, of course, with my inherently biased side of the story. The commiserating didn't satisfy me, though, didn't satisfy my need for an answer to the question I've been posing—both directly and indirectly—since I began writing about my Uber experiences: What do we owe each other? What did I owe that blind man in my car? In the very acknowledgement of his disability, did I put his blindness before his humanity, before the name on the Uber app?

I spent the rest of the day, as I have many days since leaving ESPN, wondering about my preconceptions and my misconceptions and my prejudices, my shortcomings during these nine hundred-plus Uber trips. I spent the day wondering about how we either own our truth or we deflect it, or we justify it to get from one night to the next. I spent the day wondering what it is that I have to offer, if anything, in the way of knowledge or wisdom, being that I'm a privileged, able-bodied white man who grew up a tad south of middle class, never experiencing any real prejudice, other than the upper-class, overeducated assumption that people who talk like I talk can't string together sentences like I can string together sentences.

What good would it do to try and explain to my grandmother, an eighty-something woman who had to go to a sewing room instead of high school, what these educated folks mean by "systemic racism," by "conflation of race and class," by "white imagination." I wondered how it is that I could even explain to one of the kindest women in this wide world why it is that being a pen pal with the black lady who once cleaned the insurance office where she worked, the black lady who my grandmother invited to the company Christmas party when no one else would, doesn't amount to a hill of beans, that one act of kindness doesn't begin to address centuries of inequality and oppression, doesn't begin to address why that black lady held a mop and a broom while my grandmother did her best to figure out a contraption called a computer.

I read an op-ed piece in the August 4, 2016, edition of *The New York Times*, which I still consider our country's paper of record, written by Charles M. Blow, a black man who says, "Trump is an unfiltered primal scream of the fragility and fear consuming white male America." A demographic he confines to "white men without a degree." I wondered how I should feel about that, how that implicates the majority of my extended family at a Fourth of July cookout, "white men without a degree," how that one sentence would've implicated my late father. I wondered if my father—a newspaper man himself—would have agreed with Charles M. Blow, if he would've voted for Trump or Hillary. Would a vote for Hillary even be enough to absolve them, those white men without degrees in my family? Would it even absolve me?

I read an article by Alec MacGillis and ProPublica in the latest edition of *The Atlantic*, an article about "The Original Underclass," about "white trash," as we were known and still are, about how all this Trump business might be driven more by classism than racism. I wondered if the white men without degrees around these parts (down here where Blow himself was born) have even been to a poll to take the exit exam. They could probably give a damn what color the president is, so long as they have enough Natty Ice and crystal meth to get them to tomorrow; or if they ain't drug-afflicted, then their emasculation lies not in the racial pecking order but in their lack of employment, their inability to provide for their families, their inability to pull up stakes and find a fancy job in a tall building behind a desk, up there in New York City or up there in DC, or out there in Silicon Valley, in an office with a Ping-Pong table.

Is Blow the one lacking nuance? Or am I the one doing the conflating? Perhaps the culprit isn't classism or racism at all, but rather sexism. Or must we wait until a woman runs the White House before we discuss such matters? Like the music, for example, hip-hop and rap created largely by men who look like Blow, the music that objectifies women, the music I spent much of my formative years listening to, the music I remain a fan of, couching it perhaps as voyeurism, justifying it perhaps as harmless entertainment. Although how can I ignore the absurdity of young college-age women who climb into my car and request songs that rate their worth by how much they can fit into their mouths, or songs that equate them to cocaine and dollar signs, to say nothing of the religious establishment I was raised in, that many of these young men who rap these songs were raised in, one that would not allow women at the pulpit?

Is this toxic masculinity, this misogyny regardless of color, also not a systemic problem affecting this country? Or am I conflating matters, confusing the issues, misleading the white men without degrees? Maybe we ought to just keep it black and white.

The answer lies, I imagine, somewhere in my own insecurity, in the genuine fear that with each passing Uber ride, I'm oversimplifying or overcomplicating, that I'm not able to be the blind man, nor am I able to see these topics or the people in my car from any vantage point other than my own. I worry about the validity of my unscientific polling, about whether or not I'm merely hearing the opinions of others in the relative safety that is my 2012 Honda Civic with leather interior, whether or not I'm merely offering these stories and these experiences in a space that is also relatively safe. Before I travel any farther, I must admit that while I agree with writers like Claudia Rankine, who say we mustn't conflate issues of race with issues of class with issues of gender with issues of ethnicity with issues of religion—issues that require the upmost nuance—I spend my days wondering about these matters in concert, not with the singular focus Blow would like for me to.

I must remind you of the vantage point from which my perspective has been created because if I do not remind you that these stories are filtered through the mind of one white man, do not acknowledge the limits in length and aperture of my lens, then I cannot, in good conscious, continue to tell these stories. We would all be naive to not hold our authors, to not hold our orators to a high level of accountability, to not examine with microscopic intensity their preconceptions and misconceptions and prejudices, subconscious or otherwise, before we swallow any words whole.

III

A few days after my ride with Ms. Johnson, on the Friday before the Fourth of July, I gave a young woman from Canada a ride. We'll call her "Kaley," but that isn't her real name, nor is this her confession to make, although she gave me her blessing to write about our paths crossing. Whatever thoughts you might have about faith and destiny and the universe, Kaley was my tarot card, a sign to a second chance, a chance to say all that was left unsaid between me and Ms. Johnson, between me and all my passengers up until this point. The day was warm and humid and bright, the slightest of breezes, the kind of East Tennessee afternoon I used to pray for while crammed inside a 7 train in the middle of the summer, commuting from Queens to Grand Central, eyes darting around, a forehead dotted with sweat, wishing I'd never left the A/Cs and ceiling fans and screened-in front porches of home.

It being the beginning of a holiday weekend, I was still in a slight fog from too much drinking and reminiscing the night before with old friends who are rarely in the same place at the same time anymore. So I decided to park at the airport, fewer trips per hour, time to lean back and stare at the sky, following planes as they ascended. The allure of being an Uber driver, for me at least, lies in its randomness, its lack of concern for how the makes and the models and the colors will match. I had no way of knowing when I accepted Kaley's request that she wasn't arriving, that her flight had been canceled and she was returning to a family vacation for an extra night, to a cabin in the foothills of the Great Smoky Mountains. Kaley appeared to be of Southeast Asian descent, dark hair done up in a bun: "Hi, to the Smokies," she said in a high pitch.

We had an hour-plus ride ahead of us, along winding back roads, through fields of hay and sunflowers, past creeks and barns and the houses of good country people. I asked, jokingly, "You got some stories to tell? Because we got plenty of time."

"I'm packing up my life and moving to California," she said. "I have plenty."

Like me, Kaley had left a relatively lucrative career (hers as a lawyer); but unlike me, Kaley was leaving her hometown in Canada behind instead of returning to it. She told me she'd reached an impasse, that a wider world surely awaits her, that her story surely has another twist. Kaley and I commiserated over too many hours doing something we learned we didn't love—over the loss of sleep and sanity while juggling jobs and second degrees, the loss of that certain naïveté, the kind that allows you to believe in society's construct of success, to believe that something you can fold and put in a wallet, or letters that you can capitalize and put after your name, will be what defines you. That is until you simply don't believe anymore, and you're left splayed open, forced to find a semblance of the person you thought you might be. We were self-aware enough to admit how lucky we'd been to climb the corporate ladder, the financial stability it had afforded us to make a deliberate, albeit potentially rash decision.

"It would be easier, though, wouldn't it?" Kaley said. "A nice paycheck. No more losing sleep over these silly feelings."

I glanced up in the rearview. Kaley appeared to be about my age, nearly thirty, or at least near enough to be concerned about not having a plan.

"We're not telling each other the whole truth, nothing but the truth," I said, "are we?"

"How do you mean?" Kaley asked.

"This journey we're on, it's usually about love, isn't it?" Kaley met my eyes in the rearview and smiled, a hint of recognition. "Why not tell each other everything?"

"Sure," Kaley said. "What have we got to lose?"

In that short, yet infinite window before you uncork whatever it is that would be easier left bottled up, I considered that I didn't owe anyone my truth, much less Kaley, a random woman in my car. I didn't consciously upend my life to coincide with this era of American upheaval, but I can't ignore the parallels, the uncertainty about the man I see in the mirror and the country outside my door. What do we owe each other, as Americans, as citizens of the world? I don't have an answer that satisfies me, not yet, other than to say I owe it to myself to be as honest as I can for all those times I wasn't, to be as kind as I can for all those times I took kindness for granted.

My mother tells me that I only owe the good Lord, that she hopes I'll put myself before the strangers in my car, before my readers, people who aren't always going to be there for me, no matter what I write. But still I do it, listen to their stories and tell you mine. Otherwise, what are we learning and understanding about one another besides what we already unfortunately believe we know: that in times like these, you can't really trust anybody.

Kaley and I were both untethered from our former lives, both liberated by our lack of constraints, but also unsettled by that very thing—the loss of stability in structure, the loss of comfort in conformity. When you take that kind of leap, it's impossible to land as the same person. So I'll say to you now what I told Kaley then: I'm still searching for the beginning of my story, the impetus for this journey, never certain who this man is, this man writing these words, or if I'll ever find the young man who existed before they needed to be written, if that young man can even be found.

I told Kaley I'd go first, seeing as how the idea had been mine, my guilt in need of company: "About a year and a half ago, I was on my couch in Hartford, Connecticut, staring at the ceiling. I called my girlfriend. We'd been together six years, friends for ten. I said that I was driving to Brooklyn and that we needed to talk. I said, 'I don't think I love you anymore.'"

I told Kaley about the stress of ESPN, the stress of earning an MFA on top of ESPN, the stress of the 120 miles between Hartford and Brooklyn on top of earning an MFA on top of ESPN—I'd buried my best friend under my titles and my timelines and my expectations for my career. I'd written my priority list in reverse.

"Then I dove right into a serious relationship with another woman," I said, "a woman I worked with, like the last six years could be forgotten, like they hadn't happened."

"Was the new woman already in the picture?" Kaley asked.

"The two sort of overlapped—"

I raised my hands off the wheel and slapped them down, disappointed that I couldn't go more than a few sentences without another half-truth, saving face in front of a complete stranger.

"I cheated," I said. "More than once. I lied about it. I gave her the 'it's me, not you.'"

The silence wasn't endless, wasn't awkward, as though Kaley had expected my admission, or was relieved by it. I assume Kaley could sense the messiness still festering inside me, could sense that whatever wound I'd created wasn't curable in this moment, that she was merely a witness to my guilt, simply part of an admission in the process of healing.

I've also confessed my infidelity to the people who place their trust in me, and many of them have responded with stories of their own sins, sins they protect with layers that require examining and slicing open and dissecting, sins they do not want to be viewed in black and white, or on the internet. I have been told stories by my mother, stories about her and about my father, stories that are not mine to tell, stories that she hopes will show me that my lies and infidelities are relatively minor in comparison. I have been asked why I'm holding on to this guilt, why I'm spending so much time in the past when the damage done was minimal, to hear some tell it, just a casualty of life.

Even now, though, I hesitate to absolve myself, to address any of Kaley's follow-up questions for context. She asked each one without a tinge of disgust or criticism or blame, as though she too was grateful to know another person tosses and turns, that another person stares at the ceiling at night.

"You weren't married," my mother has told me. "You didn't have kids. What is it that you think you did so wrong? Do you think you can't be a good person and still make a mistake?"

I do not believe that, just as I do not believe that context cuts one way. Context can exonerate or incriminate—every thread of dirty laundry is soiled. I could write a book about my infidelity, provide the minutiae that makes for great social media comments. Like the fact that I cheated on my girlfriend of six years while she was home in Tennessee, caring for her father who was dying of cancer. Now, that changes this confession, doesn't it?

You get to be the judge and the jury, but the gossip is not what I'm here to share, to expose the other woman, or to accuse anyone for driving me to live two lives between two women—until my girlfriend finally discovered the truth while going through texts on my phone.

What I'm here to ask are the questions I've posed to my mother in return: What are you left with once you've lost your word? What do we owe each other, especially those people who place their trust in us, if not that? What are you capable of once you've lost that?

I am not a criminal, at least not according to this society's laws, and to even write those words might seem hyperbolic to you, considering all the divorce lawyers who make a fine living. But to paraphrase some of my favorite lines ever written from the short story "Sweethearts" by Richard Ford: I do know now how you wake up one day to find yourself in the very place you said you'd never be in. And now you're not sure what's important anymore.

"Did you eventually tell her everything?" Kaley asked.

"Too late," I said. "She'd moved on, had a boyfriend, seemed happy."

I told Kaley that my confession and my apologies had become formalities, like I'd dropped them off with her mail, which was still being pushed through the slot in my front door.

"What about the other woman?" Kaley asked.

"We had a connection," I said, "but I didn't have the maturity or the decency to tell her I wasn't ready for the commitment. I'm not sure I even knew what a relationship was anymore."

I told Kaley that this new woman had to deal with demons that weren't hers to face, that I would appear and disappear from her life on a whim, leaving each time I saw in her the lying I'd done, the cheating she became emblematic of. She tried in earnest to love a man, to be honest with a man who was unable—or perhaps unwilling—to reconcile his own reflection in her eyes.

"So, enough about me," I said. "What about you?"

Kaley laughed. Because what else do you do?

"This ride was meant to be," she said. "I've been with my boyfriend for seven years, and he doesn't want to go on this journey with me."

"Does he know where your head's at?"

"We're in limbo," she said. "He likes the life we have, being close to family. He wants to settle down. And I keep thinking: Is this *it* for me?"

I told Kaley that I was only her Uber driver, but that I'd give her my two cents anyhow. "Tell him everything," I said, "and don't leave anything out. If he's going to be forever, then he'll have to hear it all anyway. Or it won't be much of a forever thing."

"Can I ask you a question?" Kaley asked.

"Do you even have to ask?" I said.

"Why'd you do it, lie to them?"

"That's my journey," I said. "All I have for you right now are a bunch of clichés, 'the grass isn't always greener' type of advice."

I told Kaley that maybe I became a bad person for a time, like you can when you lose sight of the standards you've set for yourself, when you base decisions on convenience and selfish desire. Or maybe I'd started to live life out of obligation. Maybe I didn't want marriage or the picture on the mantel, but I'd let society convince me that was all there was for me.

I told Kaley that I did love the woman I'd met in college, the woman I cheated on, two Tennessee kids who'd conquered New York City together. But love is about not giving trouble or inviting it, I said, stealing a few more lines from Ford's short story. Love is about not being in that place you said you'd never be in. Because your trouble becomes theirs, and then they're stuck trying to untangle their life from a mess they didn't ask for. You don't do that to someone you love, and so I had to redefine my definition, had to figure out what love means to me.

Kaley and I spent the rest of the ride mostly in silence—a silence of mutual respect, I believe, between two strangers who had shared a conversation about their truths. By the time we arrived at the massive corporate complex of cabin rentals in the Smokies, she'd found me on Instagram. She told me that she would follow along with my journey, anxious to read about the next chapter. We exited the car on opposite sides, and I opened the trunk and lifted out her suitcase. We shook hands, and I wished her luck.

"Best Uber ride ever," she said.

I had an hour-and-change ahead of me, along those same winding back roads, through fields of hay and sunflowers, past creeks and barns and the houses of good country people, although the sun was creeping lower and lower on the horizon, and I was alone now, in that space of my confession.

My mother is sitting opposite me behind a desk cluttered with papers. We are in a tiny trailer at her husband's used-car lot, the window A/C unit whirring. She's manning the dealership until he's back from an auction.

"Why is this so important?" she asks of my obsession with writing this down for the world to read. "What is it you think you'll accomplish?" My mother tells me that truth is for the birds on social media, that this will be whispered about at supper tables in Kingston, Tennessee, and company picnics in Bristol, Connecticut.

I recite a quote by the late author David Foster Wallace for my mother: "The truth will set you free. But not until it is finished with you." I tell her that a former ESPN colleague wrote that on my farewell card, a colleague who had known about my cheating with a coworker, a woman who did not want me to forget that the lie would follow me forever. If I've learned anything, I've learned that we enjoy spilling the secrets of others to justify our own lies. I've learned that once we lose control of our truth, it's damn near impossible to grasp it again.

My mother has been scribbling on a piece of paper. She looks up: "Where is the little boy who used to smile? When did you start spending every day so serious?"

"Why do we ever stop?" I say. Then I ask her what she once asked me: "If everyone jumped off a bridge, would you?" At what point do we decide to hold ourselves accountable out of convenience, when do our lies turn from white to gray? I ask my mother when "learning to live with" constitutes living. I don't have any delusions about my words enacting change, I tell her. But does that render them not worth writing? I don't have any delusions about the two hours I spend with kids each week at the Boys & Girls Club. I don't have any delusions about my time filling their systemic voids. But, I ask my mother, does that mean I shouldn't go and play?

She sighs and squints. She tells me that shame can break a soul. She is looking at me as a man, not her little boy. I believe my mother has accumulated responsibilities in this life—a son, a third husband, a career that is entering its last chapter—responsibilities that require a certain level of sacrifice. I believe that people who have accumulated these responsibilities want to protect their children from the pain they have experienced, from a world that isn't black and white. I believe, however, that we sometimes tell those we love what they want to hear, and in the process, we avoid the truth.

My mother and I get up from our opposite sides of the desk,

and we walk out of the cold trailer into the humid East Tennessee afternoon. I tell my mother that I do not have a wife or a child or an employer. I am ashamed of this. I tell her that the only way I can find purpose in my lack of responsibility is to write without apology, with as much truth as I can. My mother has water in her eyes. She gives me a hug. My mother, who would like to hear from her son every day, says she will give me the distance I need, that she will be here whenever I need.

"Just smile for me," she says. "Laugh every once in a while." ◆

I'd Rather Laugh with the Sinners

Around midnight on a Thursday, I roll up, window down, outside a boutique hotel in downtown Knoxville to find five white women (four brunettes and a blonde), not a dress below high-thigh, cheeks expertly rouged, lips stained cherry, each set puckered and slightly popped.

"Wait, this isn't an Uber XL," the blonde huffs.

"Come on," the youngest of the group (by my estimation) says. "We're skinny bitches."

I will later learn that this night started with a wine tasting at a chain steakhouse, a wine tasting that poured on for three hours, and then poured further into night-capping cocktails at a speakeasy in the lower bowels of the boutique hotel. I will later learn that these five women range in age from thirty to fifty and that they met at yoga, "real hot" yoga, the lowest allowable temperature being eighty-five degrees. I will soon learn that each woman is going to a separate address and that I will drop them off one by one, each one reminding me to put on my blinker and to slow down for this turn and that turn, and asking me, again and again, if I know where I'm going.

But first: "Oh. My. Goodness," the youngest chirps. "Our Uber driver is Cute. As. A. Button." She turns to the backseat: "Did you know he was as cute as a button?" She says this as she is giving me directions to the first stop, instead of simply putting the address into the Uber app, playing a game as we go, reciting the route to me, turn by turn, as though she is the woman on the GPS, mimicking her robotic accent and poorly enunciated street names. Drake raps faintly in the background.

"Can you put on something less, um, current?" a woman pipes up from the back.

"Requests?" I ask.

"Some '90s music, maybe '80s," one woman says.

"Elton John," another says.

"Billy Joel," the third says.

The other two agree, Billy Joel, and the youngest grins a big grin at me. I search for Billy Joel on my phone and cue up "Piano Man." The singing ensues and the "louder please" ensues, and the youngest, who will be dropped off first, squeezes my arm slightly, feigning sympathy, as she karaokes right along with them.

On it goes: "Uptown Girl" to "Vienna" to "She's Always a Woman." Then "Only the Good Die Young," and the eldest, who is now up front with me, wags her finger like a metronome—even though she is not keeping time to any beat that I can hear—and punctuates this invisible beat occasionally with air pistols, while the brunette in the back says, more than once, *I'd rather laugh with the sinners than cry with the saints.* "I love that fucking line, I fucking love that line."

In each driveway we linger, and they kiss on the cheeks and faux hug across the seat and ask if we can just sit for a moment and breathe in Billy Joel. The eldest is the last to go, and she and I wend our way to her home, my headlights illuminating the gated neighborhoods as we pass while Tony and Billy croon "New York State of Mind." She tells me kids are expensive and commitment is overrated. She tells me I should come to the "real hot" yoga studio and meet them at their best. After one hour and sixteen minutes and forty-two miles, she tells me that this is the most fun car ride she's ever had.

"God bless Billy Joel," she says, climbing out. "God bless Billy Joel and us five drunk bitches." She waves that metronome finger. She punches a button on her keychain and one of the three garage doors lifts. I smile and she smiles before disappearing underneath the rising door. ◆

Jack and Me
and the Prostitute

It took over a thousand trips, but I finally gave a ride to a prostitute. I didn't know the woman was a prostitute right away, just as I was ignorant then of the term "sex worker," which avoids the negative stereotypes of that other loaded word. I also didn't know she had a hookah in the small black trash bag she was carrying, tied up in a knot. I thought I was arriving at a warehouse-turned-gentrified apartment complex in downtown Knoxville to pick up the man who'd requested the ride, "Jack," although that wasn't the man's real name. I would've changed the name anyway, but that was actually what he had registered in the Uber app. I might not have ever learned the man's real name had the confusion not ensued.

When I pulled up around nine o'clock, the lights of bars and businesses and the street lamps lit up a petite, red-headed woman, who was standing in the middle of the road. She was holding a black purse and the black trash bag and talking to a man who was standing half in and half out of his black car. The man motioned to my black car, and the red-headed woman glanced at me and then back at him. She walked toward me, carefully, stilettos on a cobblestone street. I rolled down the window.

"Uber for Jack?" I asked.

"Yeah," she said and climbed in the passenger seat. "Thought the guy over there was you. He said he's an Uber too, but didn't get no call."

Her twang was thick, some sass to it. I inched the car forward.

"This for John Williams, right?" she asked.

"I thought you said it was for Jack," I said and tapped the brake.

"Well, we're on Jackson Street, ain't we?

"Wait, so you're waiting for an Uber who's picking up John?"

"I live on John Williams. What the hell you talkin' 'bout?"

I looked at the address on my phone. *John Williams Road.* "Oh," I said. "I got ya. But who's Jack?"

"I don't know who the hell Jack is."

"He's the one who called an Uber."

She made the *pssh* sound and tapped the side of my arm. "He give you a fake name."

"As long as we're on the right track," I said.

"I wouldn't go that far," she said.

I heard glass clang in the bag when she set it in the floorboard. A saxophone chirped—I'd been in a Coltrane mood.

"I'll stop all the jazz," I said.

"Don't bother me none," she said.

So I let it play, turned the dial up a notch. Before we could settle into the controlled chaos of the hi-hats and the upright bass and the unpredictable ivory, she tapped my arm again.

"I'm gonna call Jack," she said, using the man's real name. "He don't want to hear from me, cause it's about business. Well, it ain't bad."

I turned the music down to a faint drumbeat, and she dialed the number.

"Hey, Jack, so if I want to smoke the weed with the coals, you say it's gonna break the glass?" she asked. "I mean, if you smoke tobacco, then you got to be able to smoke weed." She was silent, so Jack must've been explaining his reasoning. "OK, OK. We'll see. But so you just put it in same as the tobacco? Then I can empty out the water the way you showed me how? Yeah. Yeah. OK. Next time." She hung up.

"You smoke weed?" she asked.

"I haven't in a while," I said, "but it's funny you mention it, cause a family member . . ."

"I smoke a lot," she said, not interested once I'd labeled myself a nonsmoker. "Jack has like a hookah fetish. You know what hookah is, right?" I nodded. "So he's spending like two hundred, three hundred dollars a month on these crazy-ass hookahs. So he gives me the old ones, and I smoke weed out of them."

"Better that way?" I asked.

"You know what a bong is, right?" I nodded. "So you know it has the water?" I nodded. "Well, this hookah does too, but it has coals in it too, see, that bubble up the water, like when you light a bong. And Jack's tellin' me it's gonna break the glass with weed, but it's just like a bong, ain't it? It ain't gonna break." I shrugged.

"Why do you want to empty out the water, though?"

"We smoke it with liquor. Gives the weed this taste, cause it like flavors the smoke."

"How'd you come up with that?"

"I'm a kind of connoisseur, like, you might say."

I had one hand on the wheel and the other hand resting on the gearshift. My car's an automatic, just a habit. She put a hand on my forearm.

"Try everything twice," she said. "Not once. Twice. Cause when you try it the first time, you're like already nervous and doing something you haven't done. So you're gonna be all nervous and not really, just, go at it." She took her hand off my forearm and clenched both fists and made a thrusting motion. "Everything. Twice."

"Jack's an awfully nice guy," I said, "expensive hookah, Uber rides."

"You know what Backpage is?" she asked.

I nodded. "I'm from around here," I said, "but I moved away for a while and just came back. Buddy of mine uses it."

"So, yeah—hundred fifty for an hour, fifty for half," she said. "You want my number?"

"Appreciate the offer," I said, "but I'll have to pass."

"You married?"

"No," I said. "No offense, just been trying to stay out of trouble these days."

"I see," she said. "Doesn't want it."

I hadn't been looking at her when she solicited, but I did now, and she was looking out her window, the longest she'd been silent since she got in my car. Winter had officially arrived, the high thirties, and the glass was foggy, blurring the lights of the fast-food chains and gas stations and grocery stores we were passing on a two-lane highway, headed to the rural neighborhoods on the south side of Knoxville. She made a T with her finger in the condensation, and I cranked up the defrost.

"That ain't always what it costs," she said, wiping away the T. "Jack and me's been friends a long time—seventeen years. Sometimes I don't even charge him. He pays me to watch his cats when he's away on vacation, stuff like that."

"I see," I said. "Good to have friends."

"I don't care what anybody thinks," she said. "Even my friends. I don't have many of them. You can't really trust people. I've learned that. That's why I don't have a lot friends. And even the ones who are your friends, all of them are always talking about you behind your back."

"Enemies closer," I said.

"Yeah, that's right, ain't it? Enemies closer. I figure if they're talking about me, then I'm doing something right. They're either bragging on me, or hatin' on me, and if they're hatin', then they probably wish they were doin' what I was, or jealous or something."

"Haters gonna hate," I said.

She'd rested her head back against the seat and turned toward me. She laughed and tapped my arm. "I got trust issues, I guess. That's what it really is. My brother raped me when I was thirteen. Same momma, same daddy, same house. I lived with him thirteen years, and he'd never said or did nothin' to make me think he'd do something like that."

If we're honest, there isn't anything to say to that, not an "I'm sorry," not anything. I can't empathize any more than I can imagine. To pry is to risk knowing more than you'd care to, and to question is to pick apart a memory that might very well have taken on a life far beyond its own. So I winced and shook my head and pushed out a sigh.

"It's OK," she said. "So I got trust issues. Probably why I do what

I do, huh?" She tapped my arm again. "Listen at me. Why am I opening up to you, goin' on this a way? I don't even know your name."

I didn't offer it, and she didn't come right out and ask for it.

"Can you stop at this gas station up here?"

I told her that I could and pulled in. She opened the door and the dome light shined on her, but she swiveled around before I could see her face.

"Don't leave me," she said. "I've been left before, but not by no Uber."

I said that I wouldn't, that her hookah was safe with me. She shut the door, and I was in the dark again. She walked through the fluorescent beams flickering from the gas station. She was wearing black yoga pants and a denim jacket that cut off at the waist. Her shirt wasn't any longer than the jacket, her figure as long and slender as a Virginia Slim. She had on white high-top tennis shoes, loosely tied, wide ones that accentuated her skinny calves and thighs. When she walked back around the corner in a few minutes, there was a stack of cash in one hand, a pack of Marlboros in the other, the kind with a red top.

"So how old did you say you were?" she asked as I was in reverse.

"I didn't—bet you can't guess," I said, assuming she'd peg me in my mid-twenties, like most people.

"Thirty-two," she said.

I jerked my head around. "Almost nailed it," I said. "Thirty-one." The gas station wasn't far from John Williams Road, and I was idling in the turning lane in a quarter mile, my left blinker appearing and disappearing in the dash. "How'd you know?"

"I'm always good with that kind of stuff," she said, "like maybe I ought to go to the fair, guess people's weights and stuff, like they do. So how old do you think I am?"

It was a question I never welcome from anyone, but especially not a woman, and not a woman in the South. But for some reason, I wanted to indulge her. I punched on one of the dome lights and stared into her eyes, searching them and her face. She'd been a pretty woman, no Julia Roberts, but I'm no Richard Gere. Her eyes had youth in them, blue-and-green speckled. Her hair was below her shoulders, and she had bangs. It was like she'd mixed and matched certain styles of certain times, like she was her own era. The cigarette wrinkles gave her away, and the crow's feet. Probably mid-forties, but I didn't offer a guess, not yet. She shifted her eyes downward and her cheeks flushed a bit, embarrassing me, embarrassing a prostitute.

I punched off the dome light. I made the "*thirrrr*" sound. "OK," I said, "I really don't—"

"Forty-four," she said. "Couldn't have guessed, right?"

"You look good," I said.

We were in a neighborhood now, curving through farmland, no street lights. I clicked on my high beams.

"So all you do is drive Uber?" she asked.

"For now," I said. "Life got out ahead of me. Had to catch up to it."

"Life, tell me about it," she said. "I'm there right now, you don't even know."

Gravel crunched beneath my tires, and I turned into her driveway, which stretched a few hundred yards into a field, the farmhouse stark against a backdrop of pastures that would be a dried-out green against the blue sky come morning. The car bounced over potholes. There was a garage that didn't appear to be in use, a beat-up purple

Ford Ranger parked in front of it. She had me pull around back, where a porch light was on.

"Sure you don't want my number?" she asked. "Must be lonely, catching up to life."

I was lonely, I have been, and I am still. No denying that. Probably in my eyes. I nearly said yes. I nearly asked her if she'd take fifty an hour just to stop by and talk, have a beer, listen to some Coltrane. Maybe she'd like jazz.

I've always been more comfortable around people who lack pretense, who haven't swallowed their id, that human instinct to do what perhaps we've all wondered about, what we've all imagined. People like that can often be as genuine as a kid, if they can sense you're human too, like them, if they can see in your eyes that the straitjacket of society is probably the only thing keeping you on the right track. (Although there I go again, assuming we all have the same choice in the matter.)

Sitting here now, drinking a beer under the harsh yellow of the light above my dining room table, I wish I would've put her number in my phone. I would've paid fifty an hour to talk, to hear why it went one way instead of the other, even if she couldn't make complete sense of it. There are people out there who would tell her that it's never too late to change, but I'd just listen, ask her if she had a favorite book, what liquor made her weed taste the best. We'd have a beer or three, and then I'd drive her back to John Williams Road.

But you and I both know that isn't the way this is set up, that this isn't *Pretty Woman*, that when she climbed out of my car there in that pasture, she was the prostitute again, and I was me, not Jack, and Jack would see her before too long. ◆

Go West, Young. . . Man?

PART 1

When you're pragmatic, taking a year off from life, even when you have the money in the bank, goes against your very being, that voice in your head that says you should always be saving to weather the rainy days that are surely ahead. So ever since I said fuck it and set out from Knoxville for the Grand Canyon on September 7, 2016, winding up in San Francisco, twenty-five hundred miles from home, I've been overthinking and over-writing and over-questioning with each new hotel and each night spent in a friend's spare room in each new city. It's September 12 now, and I'm sitting in a coffee shop on Santa Monica Boulevard, humming Sheryl Crow and wishing I could just have some fun.

I am not the first person to embark on this pilgrimage, nor will I be the last person to eat or to pray or to try and love again. My sins are not original, nor are my rhetorical questions profound. Socrates has asked them all before, as have many, many men and women after him, most of them a lot smarter than I.

But when exactly did we decide that life's great questions have a shelf life?

"Why are we here?" is the copyrighted existential question; although "Why do we get to do what we do and earn what we earn for it while we are here?" is perhaps the question we'd all prefer to have answered. Why is one person wearing his or her shoes and not mine? Why do I have the luxury of sitting in a coffee shop on Santa Monica Boulevard, pecking away at my "problems" on a MacBook Air? There are those who'd say I should spend this year reading those smarter folks, like Socrates, who have already dug for answers till they've hit an inevitable root. And while I am doing some reading and some learning from the great thinkers, I can't fathom what books will do for me without any experience. This is my *Good Will Hunting* year, my year to smell the inside of the Sistine Chapel for myself. What good can I do anyone if all I know is what someone else said between two covers?

The "truth" behind why I'm driving people around, why I drove all the way to the Pacific Ocean, well, that remains ever-elusive, a "truth" I will continue to explore, but one that I believe lies somewhere on this quixotic quest of mine, this quest to determine what "true happiness" looks like to me, whether it is even achievable for me, for anyone really. Or if true happiness is and always will be dictated by the nature and by the nurture and by the circumstances that coalesce in order to "know thyself"—if true happiness is, in the end, predetermined; if it is, God forbid, beyond our control.

As an Uber driver, I cross paths with so many people who aren't chronicled here, mostly because they are less slices of life than slivers, but glimpses nonetheless that remain lodged in my memory. Not until these snapshots have been examined, not until I've discerned how they alter my perspective, can I begin to decipher the signs and make sense of the road map. Sitting in another coffee shop, just west of San Francisco on Ocean Beach, the Pacific breeze blowing through, I'm reminded of Darius and of Tim and of Matt—three men I drove around Knoxville on separate days, three men who have nothing more in common than their chromosomes and the coincidence that they spent a few miles in my car. I have thought about them often since dropping them off, what turns their paths have taken, why theirs crossed with mine.

On a Friday around noon, at a health-care facility near downtown Knoxville, I picked up Darius, a young black man with a clean, short fade and goatee who'd just finished peeing in a cup, hoping to begin his new job on an assembly line. Darius, who was wearing khaki slacks and a navy hoodie, told me he was so relieved to finally be on salary, that he was worn out with sixty-plus-hour weeks as a stock boy at two different grocery stores. He'd arrived in Knoxville from Atlanta four years ago, a twenty-year-old with nothing in his bank account, needing those long hours to pay for his one-bedroom apartment, to put food in his refrigerator and clothes on his back, maybe even splurge on a cable package that would allow him to keep up with his favorite sports teams back home. I could sense the enthusiasm in Darius's voice, the speed at which he explained how he would start out at fifteen dollars per hour, with the promise of a raise in six months, with the promise of overtime pay for every hour beyond forty. Darius told me he was single, no kids, that he'd have enough left over from his check to save for a reliable car, maybe even splurge on a flat-screen to watch the Falcons and the Braves and the Hawks.

"I left Atlanta cause my boys were movin' weight, makin' it the wrong way," Darius said, referring to the drug trade. "Only legit job I could get was as a janitor, and I didn't want to clean up after nobody. I had to leave the scene. Knoxville's quiet. Not got all that noise. My boys back home, they ask me why I work my ass off for nothin'. But it'll pay—hard work pays off."

I smiled to keep from wincing, to keep from letting my doubt show, to push down the pain that flares up when what you've seen out in this world is in direct opposition to Darius, this young man who has, against society's odds, seemingly worked his ass off to outrun the caricature of other young black men like him, his reward an assembly line. I let my mind wander to the Socratic questions, to why Darius had his safety net pulled out from under him, while I grew up in a family that didn't have much extra, but one that would allow me to land softly, should my outsized dreams never pan out. I let my mind wander to Darius's "true happiness"—if his definition is simply to have a reliable car and to watch the Falcons on a flat-screen and to turn screws as they pass on an assembly line instead of picking up and setting down boxes filled with canned goods.

I dropped Darius off at Kroger for his ten-hour shift, nothing but his backpack and his one-bedroom apartment and all that's in it to his name. "Good luck," I said, the harsh truth being that luck, not working his ass off, is about all that will move this young black man into a higher tax bracket. Darius raised his chin, a reverse nod, and flashed his index and middle fingers spread wide. And I thought, if only we could find it.

Three days later, on a Monday, around 5:00 in the evening, I arrived at a one-story brick house about ten minutes from downtown

Knoxville to pick up Tim, a bespectacled, middle-aged, clean-shaven white man with thinning brown hair. He was standing in his front yard wearing an untucked, unbuttoned, short-sleeve polo and knee-length shorts, hands on his hips, smoking a cigarette. He was squinting into the yellow sun, into the clear blue sky. A beat or two passed before he acknowledged that I was parked in his driveway. Tim took a deep, last pull and stomped his cigarette out on the concrete.

He climbed in, and I asked how his day had been through the rearview. Tim mumbled, nearly inaudible: "Fine—still here." I assumed he was in no mood to talk, so I cued up some unobtrusive indie music on Spotify and started the trip.

"Well . . . ," Tim said. I raised my eyebrows in the rearview. "How 'bout you?" he asked, forceful enough to rise above the music. I lowered the volume.

"Alright," I said, "just tryin' to make a few bucks."

"What it's all about, ain't it?" he said, his voice a mumble again.

"Wish it wasn't," I said, "but it's a fact we can't escape, hard as we try."

"Sad that some are better at it than others," he said. "Probably make things a lot easier, if we could all just be equal."

The complexity within the simplicity of Southern men is something I missed while living up North. It's the osmosis of emotions through a single phrase, how every word is pushed out through the pressures of the Bible Belt, which is always cinched tight around our waists, no matter how far we might travel from God's country.

"There was a time when I was good at it," I said. "But I decided it wasn't for me."

"Why in the hell would you quit being good at making money?" Tim asked, slapping his hands down on his knees for effect.

Man in the (Rearview) Mirror

That monologue had arrived, the one that I tend to steer clear of, the one that I have down pat, the one where I have to joke away my Existential Crisis, to justify why it is that I left a W-2 that a lot folks will never see, those people who were destined for a certain tax bracket before they ever even filed. Tim nodded a couple of times in the rearview while I attempted to relate the reasons for my exit from ESPN, although he grunted at one-liners like "I'd lost myself behind a desk"; "What I was doing with my life didn't satisfy me"; "Being married to a career doesn't make the bed warm at night." I don't blame his skepticism, don't expect him or you to empathize or to sympathize with my plight.

"What about you?" I asked. "You any good at makin' money?"

"Same job for twenty-five years," Tim said. "'Bout to lose it, though. I run a distribution company that's getting farmed out to a bigger company. The son of the dead owner thinks they can save money. They can't, but he's a tech kid. He thinks he knows numbers. People have worked there for forty years, and I'm gonna have to let 'em go, to tell 'em we're shuttin' down. What do they do now? What do I do? I have to type up a résumé for the first time in my life."

It all coalesced now, at least the nature and the circumstance. Tim was of the old school, the company-loyalty generation. I was driving him for that drink or three downtown on a Monday evening, the one(s) that you have as you reflect on all you could've been doing instead of being loyal to a company that inevitably lumped you in with the bottom line. Tim was in the wallowing stage, a state of mind that doesn't deal in small talk, a state of mind that you can't poke at or prod without a warrant, because at that point that perspective is the only one that makes any sense, all a man like Tim believes he has left.

But I risked it anyway, cause what do I have if nothing else to lose:

"Could be a clean slate," I said.

"Could be," Tim said. "But clean slates don't pay much, do they? How you gettin' by, anyway?"

I told Tim that I'd counted my pennies in my twenties. I told him that I'd grown up around a grandmother who'd only buy a gallon of Mayfield's if it was on sale and around a grandfather who wouldn't eat out because he said the only restaurant with any return on the dollar was the Shoney's buffet and around a mother who picked up part-time jobs to keep her teenage son in overpriced school clothes so he could fit in. But I told Tim that living every day like somebody might take it away can wear on a person, that spending all of my twenties around men who were worried about the size of their direct deposits and their place in the corporate pecking order doesn't add up to much perspective, that when those are the only men you have to look up to, then, well, that kind of mentality doesn't offer much peace of mind.

I told Tim about leaving the United States for the first time, at thirty-one years old—of Ireland, of driving on the left side of the road, of communing with the sheep, of nights at pubs in towns that weren't on maps; of Bonnaroo, of all those kids who didn't seem to care much about color or creed, just the music; of my return to Connecticut and to New York, of my ghosts; and of my upcoming trip out West, possibly all the way to the Pacific. And finally of Italy, of my trip to smell the inside of that chapel, to look up at that ceiling for myself.

"Easy to say when you're young and don't have anyone to worry about," Tim said.

"You got a partner?" I asked.

"No," he said.

"Kids?"

"No kids," he said. "But I've got a mortgage and a car payment. I've got responsibilities."

Tim was in no mood for me to test his logic, for me to question what exactly his house and his car amount to in his life. We'll all write and rewrite our priority lists in our own time, and most of us ain't on the same schedule.

"You know what I'd do," Tim said, "if I were you. I'd drive the Pacific Coast Highway—I'd take as many days as I wanted, stop every chance I got."

"You could do it," I said. "That house payment and that car payment will be here when you get back."

Tim didn't respond to that, and I can commiserate. I know the layers that have to be peeled back before you can face these questions I'm asking, to perform an audit of your life, an audit that can undermine whatever stability you've created, that stability and structure we need in order to roll out of bed every morning. Tim must've decided that all he wanted to entertain on this Monday evening was a stiff drink, perhaps a pretty barmaid who might not poke or prod at his logic, or who at least had a prettier face than mine.

Tim didn't reverse nod, or throw up his index and middle fingers. He just walked out onto Market Square, headed to find whatever peace he could, in however many drinks he'd decide would offer comfort, however cold. I'm not a judge or a jury—I've known plenty of days when Tim's version of "happiness" was my own, when it seemed so far out of reach that if tomorrow decided not to come, then the bottom of a bottle was as good a place as any to wait.

• • •

The next day, a Tuesday, around the same time in the afternoon, I picked up Matt at a hotel downtown. Matt was in for business, a pharmaceutical sales manager from a small town in North Carolina. He was a bespectacled, balding white man himself, although he was wearing slacks and his Oxford was tucked in, and he looked much younger than Tim—or perhaps it was the grin, that enthusiasm for life that has a way of softening a man's eyes, adding a sheen to his cheeks. I'd obviously never met Matt, but he was immediately engaging when he climbed in, like two old buddies reuniting for dinner.

Matt's questions were so rapid-fire that I could barely answer one before another. He wanted to know how long I'd been Ubering, how I'd known precisely where to be even though the app had dropped the pin in the wrong place. He wanted to know what I did when I wasn't Ubering, and he didn't skip a beat when I told him about my exit from ESPN, about my passion for storytelling, about my Existential Crisis, about believing—perhaps in my egotism or perhaps in my naïveté —that I have something to say to the world worth hearing.

"I love to read," Matt said, "especially writers whose stories make me think. I was a philosophy major, believe it or not. The Lord put me on a different path, but I still like to consider why anything is the way it is, hear how another person thinks about it."

I was surprised that Matt mentioned philosophy and the Lord in the same sentence, to hear him say that he wanted to read anything that might be in direct opposition to what the Good Book says. I've long considered the two—philosophy and religion—mutually exclusive, always thought that someone who entertained "Why are we here?" or "why bad things happen to good people" would eventually philosophize himself or herself out of believing there is any one true answer to what might exist beyond this life. But that is admittedly my own shortsightedness, to assume that someone can't both question blind faith while also remain steadfast in it.

It is not a discussion for the faint of heart: what our purpose is here, where we go when we die, why it is that we were given the chance to hang around any longer than the next person. But if I'm honest, I was envious of Matt, of the fact that I might never be as genuinely content or as genuinely certain as Matt seemed to be with whatever life puts him through, that whatever questioning he might do he has found some peace within his purpose, or at least with who is moving his plot forward. When Matt learned that I'd published a few short stories and that I was writing about my Uber experiences on my website, he was eager to read my work. But he said that he'd abstained from any social media outlets other than LinkedIn. I told him that he could find me there too, so he immediately "connected" with me, and he laughed when he read my current title of "Existential Mess."

"I know all about that existential journey," Matt said. "Keep writing. Maybe you'll be the next great philosopher."

Matt never asked about my higher power, about what or whom I believe in. Matt did not profess to me, did not express concern for me as a man. He was simply glad to meet me, interested in what I had to offer. He encouraged me to search, even if I might not find an answer, much less his answer. Matt never mentioned having a wife or children, only that he had a sister who'd married a poet.

"I wish I was that type of creative," he said. "Life might've turned out a lot different."

But Matt said that he's just fine with pharmaceutical sales, that he's happy, that he was just looking forward to having sushi, maybe a beer, with his client that night. To hear Matt tell it, sushi and a beer and a conversation are reason enough to smile.

I'm home now, back in Knoxville, in my own coffee shop, my eight-cup percolator sputtering as I write. I'm back from that land where caricatures of men become manifest, where they tip ten-gallon hats and wear cowboy boots and bolo ties without a hint of irony. It's September 25, the day before the first presidential debate between Donald Trump and Hillary Clinton, nearly a week since I drove the twenty-five hundred miles back through Lake Tahoe and Zion National Park, stopping in Fayetteville, Arkansas, to eat lunch with a friend I hadn't seen since middle school. He'd been following my road trip on Facebook.

I'd never been one to take much stock in signs, or in the following of them. To do so takes believing in the old adage "Everything happens for a reason." But when you become an Uber driver, ignoring signs and disobeying them can be bad for business—and when you're on a journey like I'm on, when how you spend every minute of every day is your choice and yours alone, you can't help but start to wonder why anything happens, why anyone climbs into your car, or why anyone appears in your Facebook timeline.

Exactly one month ago today, I woke up and said good morning to my laptop and scrolled through various news outlets before my inevitable turn to Facebook, which had plopped in my timeline a post by Dale Partridge. I was not familiar with Partridge until that Thursday morning, although I probably should've been. In 2011, the same year my then-girlfriend and I moved from New York City to Hartford and shared a postal address for the first time, Partridge cofounded Sevenly, an apparel company that gives seven dollars back to charity with each purchase. The company cleared a million in its first year, when Partridge was just twenty-six. The company (named Sevenly because it rhymes with *heavenly*) boomed, and Partridge was divined a social start-up wunderkind—until Facebook altered its algorithms in 2013 and Sevenly's business model was disrupted, its stock price hit, causing baby-boomer stockholders to question whether Partridge's bottom-line savvy was being overshadowed by his charitable intentions. Less than a year later, Partridge was fired, as a twenty-nine-year-old millionaire.

In the years since, Partridge has reinvented his pride and become a stay-at-home author, family man, and motivational speaker, "teaching leaders and organizations how to position their brand, love their people, and develop profitable corporate social responsibility programs." On April 10, 2016, Partridge turned thirty-one, twelve days before me. Partridge has a wife and two children, a boy and a girl. Here is the opening line of Partridge's post, the one he paid Facebook to incorporate into its algorithms, the one that found its way into my timeline: "I'm not sure when men decided that 30 was the new 15," Partridge writes, oblivious to the fact that fifteen was the very age that I lost my father. Partridge continues: "Our culture has a boy problem. In Italy, they call it Peter Pan Syndrome. I call it immaturity and selfishness. Men so focused on their dreams, their visions, and their desires they find themselves wealthy, known, and alone."

Partridge says this America needs men "who hold a moral code and [do] not compromise it. [Men] who love women, treat them as they would their own daughters and lead them when everything doesn't make sense." Partridge, whose Facebook author page has more than 400,000 "followers," who is white like me and calls himself a "Business Person" and a "Follower of Christ," writes in another post that prior to Sevenly he was relatively broke, which he defines as living in an apartment with some debt and making forty-eight thousand dollars a year, "nowhere near a net worth of $1 million." This is the first time in all of these essays that I'm concerned about lines being drawn, between Partridge and me and you. I'm concerned about putting words in Darius's mouth, telling you what a young black man would give to make forty-eight thousand dollars a year, what he would give to have the education to start a company that would make him a millionaire. I'm concerned about assuming why Tim can't bear to return to a salary as low as forty-eight thousand dollars a year, to assume why he does not have a wife or child, if he would agree with Partridge's definition of a man. I can't begin to assume that Matt would be happy with forty-eight thousand dollars a year, or if he would be happy if it was what the Lord intended, if perhaps Matt does not have a wife or a child for reasons that Partridge cannot fathom, reasons that Partridge has been afforded the luxury of not having to face.

I'm wondering if I need to repeat for you lines like "[men] who love women . . . and [who will] lead them when everything doesn't make sense." What's your definition of a man? What doesn't "make sense" to Partridge? Is it those men who don't love women in our America, the ones who were senselessly murdered in an Orlando nightclub? Is it Hillary Clinton being a leader of men that doesn't make sense to Partridge? Or maybe it's men like Darius and Tim and Matt and myself who don't make sense to Partridge, the men who do not have wives and do not have children, the men who do not have that nuclear portrait on the mantle, whose next Christmas likely won't be spent in expensively woven, brightly colored sweaters, sending out cards adorned with our surnames in calligraphy.

I'm not sure whether or not I should have more respect for Partridge, if perhaps he is the lion and I am the sheep, biblically speaking. Because he is firmly drawing the line behind which he stands, firmly espousing what he believes to be the definition of a man, while I am tilting at windmills, trying to examine all sides, the whys of Darius and of Tim and of Matt and of myself, instead of getting in line with what society expects of me—to love women blindly and lead them now, especially now, when everything doesn't "make sense."

We are a nation that has prided itself on the separation of church and state, yet a nation whose citizens bring whatever ideology they believe defines them to the polls. It's the ultimate display of hypocrisy. We are a nation at odds with itself because its citizens are conflicted with what it means to be an American, to be a man and to be a woman, a nation conflicted with the idea that speaking English and believing in Christianity and practicing heterosexuality are requisites for a Social Security number. Like our nation, I too am conflicted. Maybe Partridge is right about me. Maybe when I fly to Italy in a couple of weeks, to drink more expensive espresso, the Italian men there will tell me I am Peter Pan, that I've pushed away three women thus far because I'm afraid to grow up.

A friend and former ESPN colleague, an editor and writer and father of three whom I highly respect, recently read the essay in which I admit to cheating on my girlfriend of six years. He told me that he sees "a man seeking a deeper truth through the prism of his failed relationships." He worries I won't find truth that way. He told me that he worries I'll only grow to hate myself. When my friend told me that I must "mark" my limitations as a man and learn from them,

I imagined a child's drawings, those drawings in which we, as children, color outside the lines, make our clouds orange and our sun blue, those drawings that our parents applaud, hang on the refrigerator, chalk up to creativity. When and why does coloring outside the lines and making our clouds orange and our sun blue become problematic, become a marking of "limitations" that can no longer be displayed on a refrigerator? When do those markings become something we keep hidden for fear that it might render us different, less of a man, or perhaps not able to fit into society's norms?

I'm not so sure that there is a discernible second part to Socrates's advice, the part that advises you how to proceed once you've gotten to "know thyself," his advice for when you realize that "thyself" is simply a product of the nature and the nurture and the circumstances you were given. While I can't claim to have read all he wrote, Socrates doesn't seem to have instructed us on exactly what to do with our "limitations," with our inability to live up to Partridge's standards of a man, of society's standards of a man. Socrates did not bother to tell us what to do when society finally decides to break it to us—that the sun is yellow, the clouds are white, and the sky is blue; that, as Partridge might say, men should love women and men should lead women; and that forty-eight thousand dollars a year and a roof over your head, at least to hear Partridge tell it, ain't worth a million.

My mother has said more than once that maybe I ought to talk to someone, that maybe a pill, just to take the edge off, might not be a bad idea until I get through whatever this "thing" is, this thing I keep calling my Existential Crisis. I wonder what Socrates would think of that, needing a pill to live with "thyself," to keep the sun yellow and the clouds white and the sky blue. A few months before I put in my two weeks' notice at ESPN, a former boss told me that he didn't believe "true happiness" was in the cards for me. He was worried about my pessimism having morphed into misery, into a palpable hatred for life. In the moment, I thought what a cold-hearted statement to make to another person. But perhaps there was some truth to his psychoanalyzing; perhaps there will always be the Matts of the world, those who are predisposed to be "truly happy," and then there is me, the one put here to question it.

I hadn't thought about the exchange with my former boss since it'd happened, nearly a year ago—not until I woke up after a Labor Day weekend cookout at a friend's house, a man I've known since we were boys. I woke up on his couch, in the haze of a hangover, and through the cobwebs I could see him on the opposite couch, watching *SportsCenter*, catching up on the scores from college football's opening weekend. I could hear his wife blow-drying her hair, getting ready for church. Then his three-year-old daughter stomped into the living room wearing tiny heels and a dress, wanting her daddy to see how pretty she was in her Sunday school outfit. It's a tableau that seemed so far out of reach then and even now, a tableau of what my life perhaps could've been, if I'd been more like Partridge's definition of a man.

Maybe all this soul searching is nonsense. Maybe I'll never be Matt without a pill. I'll never be Darius, because I've not known what it is to be a color other than white. I wonder if Partridge would say my drive across the country, up the Pacific Coast Highway, was a childish thing to do, a symptom of Peter Pan Syndrome. I wonder if Tim will ever make that drive, if he'll let go of whatever version of "thyself" he thinks he should've been or could've been; if he'll find himself anew; if he'll find happiness, somewhere out there along that picturesque body of water, under the blue sky and the white clouds and the yellow sun. ◆

A Rookie's Guide
to the Grand Canyon

Two cents' worth: Should you ever find your way to the Grand Canyon, don't ignore the National Park Service when it clearly states on the signs that the Hermit Trail is "for experienced desert hikers," and that it is an "unmaintained trail" that drops "2,000 vertical feet in the first 2.5 miles"—two thousand vertical feet that you will have to hike back up.

If you must, then start your day with more sustenance than two cups of coffee and a granola bar, and wear something besides Nikes. Don't ignore the NPS when it clearly states to carry "at least two gallons of water." If you must still, then wear a hat and don't assume that five-mile runs three or four times a week are equivalent to a twelve-mile round-trip hike that bleeds into the afternoon, when there is no escaping that orange-red Arizona sun. If on you must trek, then for Christ's sake, stop at Santa Maria Spring, rest, realize that those boulders you scaled in the middle of what is called the "trail" won't be so easy to go up and over. In fact, turn around and catch the bus to the tourist entrance, where you just look over the rail and gasp.

But if I know anything, I know what it is to see for yourself. And so when you get to Cope Butte, let reality set in. Stand on the edge of that cliff and understand that you're not sure which way is up or which way is down, only that the Grand Canyon has swallowed you. Retreat. Ration water and the chicken salad sandwich you bought way back at the visitor center, when you were going to show all those tourists, gasping over the rail. The Cathedral Stairs will own you, and you will become friends with every crevice and every crag and every piece of shale because it is just you and them, no cell service, no other hikers for miles. The thoughts you had been thinking will cease—just you and the shale and the lizards and the buzzing sounds. The out-of-body experience will come on slowly, once the "trail" tricks you and you hit the edge of another cliff that only goes into the abyss. You must embrace this. You must externalize your inner monologue for motivation. You must go *Training Day* Denzel and say audibly, with no one within earshot, "King Kong ain't got shit on me." Because you will still have the two thousand vertical feet to ascend, and your half bottle of water will be warm, something to wet the dryness.

You will survive because you don't want to be the one who has the rangers scale down and show you the map that says the Hermit Trail is "for experienced desert hikers." You will survive and you will walk to the concession stand at Hermit's Rest, and you will consider all the awful things you might do to someone for a Powerade, all the awful things you want to do to the lady who is holding up the line because she no longer wants the can of cold liquid on the counter. You hear her tell the clerk that she does not drink anything with high-fructose corn syrup. You will lick what salt is left around your lips, and you will be too tired to go ballistic.

You will eventually get your Powerade, and you will retire to a shady spot near the railing overlooking the Colorado River, which you know is there but cannot discern. You will smile and chug your Powerade, and you will whisper, "You win." ◆

Go West,
Young. . . Man?

PART 2

Every word I've ever written has been for my father, not for any audience or any paycheck. I realize now that he is the reason for this public display of soul-baring. My father was fifty-nine when I was born, a man I've always assumed wanted another child to correct any imperfections he might've had as a father to my much older brother and sister, who were the children of a much younger man, perhaps a man who had yet to learn from his mistakes. He was semiretired when I came along, a self-made man who'd earned a better-than-decent living as an editor and part-owner of three small-town East Tennessee newspapers—even coming out of retirement in the early '90s to be the editor-in-chief of a fourth—back when words in ink were the only true source of information, a community's only true source of record, of "real" news.

When I lived in a condo in Hartford, Connecticut, the only home I've ever owned, I displayed a black-and-white photo of my father in his late thirties or early forties, the man I never knew, someone else's father. I did this, I believe, because it was easier than staring at a color photo of the man I do remember, the one I believe would be disappointed in me, in some of the things I've related in these essays. That black-and-white man has a long, handsome jaw-line. He is wearing a dark suit with a skinny tie—the ones that have since come back into style and may already be out again—and he has a pipe in his mouth. He has the crispest flattop I have ever seen. I like to look at that black-and-white photo every once in a while and pretend I can ask that man his regrets, his outlook on the life ahead. I like to pretend that I can ask that man what he thinks of the man I've become, if he thinks my father, his older avatar, would be proud.

My father was of another generation, of an era when picking up a person on the side of the road was the polite thing to do, no matter who they might be voting for, a time when a cup of coffee or a beer and a story was what passed for entertainment on the front porch. To my knowledge, he never left this country, although my mother thinks he might have spent a stint abroad while serving his four years in the military, jumping out of airplanes, a basic-training instructor during World War II. When the army tried to convince my father to stay, to be a career military man, he put a nickel in the jukebox at Ft. Bragg in North Carolina and played a song I cannot remember the name of, only that it was a sad one, and he said to them, "Boys, I'm going home to Tennessee."

He rarely left the state after that. He told me that he flew to New York City once on business, but instead of hanging around to see the sites, he hopped in the cab and went straight to the airport. I never heard about my father driving the Pacific Coast Highway or peering down into the Grand Canyon, but he was an asset to Kingston, Tennessee. He told the stories of its people in the newspaper. He was the public address announcer at high school football games (the press box bears his name today) and the clock operator at basketball games. He was the man who folks, both black and white, would call when they needed a loan to help pay a month's mortgage, right up until he had to tell them that he was doing well to pay his own bills. My father was a Democrat who served as a Republican press secretary in the Tennessee state capitol during the 1980s. He would drive about anyone anywhere for free, would listen to their stories for sustenance, would ask questions instead of proselytizing because he believed that was how you learned something, that was what you owed a fellow American.

My father typed a letter to me dated April 19, 1998, and gave it to me three days later, the day I became a teenager:

> You are a very delightful young man: a good student, a good athlete and most importantly, a person of good character and judgment. I am confident you will retain the latter and grow up to be a real asset to the community in which you choose to live. . . . You will be what you will be by the company you keep or, better said, the friends you choose for yourself.

My father wrote that life would be enjoyable and profitable if I continued to follow what I knew to be the right road, and not leave it for temporary acceptance by those who could lead me astray. He told me to continue to believe in the Lord.

Two and a half years later, in December 2000, my father stepped awkwardly off the sidewalk as he was leaving one of my high school basketball games. He hit his head on the concrete. His brain would unknowingly begin to hemorrhage, and he would eventually go into a coma, a coma that would last a week before we pulled the plug and brought that seventy-four-year-old man home to his one-story, red-brick house atop a steep hill in Kingston, Tennessee, the place where he would've wanted to die.

Most all of his life, my father was known as "Boots," a nickname given to him as a kid for no other reason than that's what came out when his infant brother tried to say "LaRue," or so the legend goes. The other half of the legend goes that his mother had a friend whose surname was LaRue, and she liked the sound of it so much that she adopted it for her second-to-last child. My parents named me for my father to carry on the legacy, but I have fallen so utterly short of the legacy and that letter's promise. I have a résumé that would impress many, yet I have not been an asset to any community in which I've chosen to live, save for maybe that campus in Bristol, Connecticut, all those hours I poured into a paycheck and my own self-worth. I am still not an asset to any physical community, but I believe I am an asset to the community of social media, where these stories first found life—the space of our twenty-first century day-to-day, where, to hear some tell it, words of any real substance need not be wasted.

A friend of mine from grad school told me that he is proud of me, proud of my growth as a writer, proud of my soul searching and my seeming honesty, but that as a fellow writer, he isn't completely convinced of my truth-seeking. He told me after reading the essay in which I confessed my infidelities that he wondered if my "truth" wasn't simply a version to be written now on the internet and to be edited later, for a space that could handle a more realistic "truth," for a space where I could ponder how I affected the lives of those two women, how the "truth" has affected me. He said that he believed I was an editor by nature, questioned whether I was actually after the "truth" or just pandering to a willing audience.

He is right about one thing: I am searching for the perfect version of every post and every essay. I am doing my damnedest to keep the camera lens pointed squarely at myself. Because, as writers, we often confuse the salaciousness of the details, the confessions of sins with "truth," with an understanding of humanity. Sure, any story of our lives is ours to tell, yet these words, when read by the women I've slept with or by my mother and my grandmother, can have unintended consequences. The "truth" doesn't have to inherently hurt.

A woman I met recently, a woman who is about my age, sent me a message via Facebook and told me that she started reading my website from the beginning, that she was inspired to start her own journey following a marriage that had ended over infidelity, although she had been the one cheated on. I have heard writers say that their pursuit is to touch even one person, regardless if that person is a paying customer. And while I can't speak for them, I can speak for myself. I can tell you that her direct message is reason enough for me to wake up and write some more, that all I've ever hoped for was to make someone else believe in his or her story, to believe that it is worth telling, on whatever platform. I believe my father would agree with that. He would be proud of these essays, although not what prompted them. I believe he would admire me for driving people around, albeit for a fee, although he would probably worry about me out here alone, in times like these, much like my mother.

On Saturday, October 8, 2016, I will board a plane from Nashville, Tennessee, to Charlotte, North Carolina, and then fly to Rome. It'll be just my second time outside the United States. My first was in early May of this year, when I flew from JFK to Ireland and drove on the left side of the road from Shannon to Dublin, swerved out of more than one roundabout, poured a Guinness from behind a bar in Fishertown, and stood on the opposite shore of the Atlantic Ocean, seriously contemplating whether I could create a new life back where I'd left my old one.

Man in the (Rearview) Mirror

I do not know why my father never left this country. I can't understand what causes a man to have so much pride in a town, to the point that it pains him to leave. I do not know who my father would have voted for in the 2016 presidential election. He did not live to see a black man become president, and I do not know how he would feel about a woman being in the Oval Office. I was fifteen the last time I saw my father. Fifteen is young, but fifteen can also feel like a grown man. I am thirty-one now, and I miss my father more than I ever did then, would give a lot to hear his voice again. I realize now that the "truth" I am seeking is what kind of man I've become, having to face that "truth" without his approval, or his forgiveness.

My father did not live to see Facebook, either, and I do not know what he would say about social media, how it has affected our society and his lifelong profession of journalism. I do not know what he'd think of a video in my Facebook timeline this week, a video of a young black man giving "free hugs" to police officers wearing riot gear in Charlotte, the place where I will layover for about an hour, as if there is nothing to see. This young man is being screamed at by other black people, being called a traitor, being told he is just another "n---a" to these officers. And then tear gas is fired off camera, perhaps gunshots, and the camera shakes and the person filming starts running, as does the young man giving free hugs.

I do not know what my father would think of this, what he would think of those black people having to resort to protest, the fact that we've let their words and their stories go unheard, the fact that anyone would have to give out hugs for free. But the man I've become can't help but wonder: How can we blame anyone but ourselves?

I believe my father would agree with that. ◆

Nerds Need Love Too

Around nine at night, I idle outside the main entrance to the shopping mall on the east side of Knoxville. It is one of two malls in Knoxville, the other being on the west side of town, about twenty minutes away. The mall on the east side is less frequented, a place that people on the west side don't go out of their way to visit, whereas people on the east side will make a special trip to the west side for dinner at The Cheesecake Factory, or to have the cracked screen on their iPhone 5s fixed at the Apple Store. At the mall on the east side, there is a Chinese buffet, Mandarin Palace, and a Mythic Airbrush, where you can get a custom T-shirt, perhaps emblazoned with a blood-red heart, an arrow piercing it, your true love's initials etched on either side. Or a Southern phrase: "Bless your heart," perhaps.

On the east side of town, as I wait for "Aaron" to show up, I look out over the three-quarters empty parking lot and think about the multiple shootings that have occurred here, dating back to when I was a kid, incidents that have created an invisible barrier around this mall, buttressed by stigma and stereotypes over decades. I'd texted Aaron when I arrived, but no response. So I call. After several rings, I'm transferred to the voice mailbox of a woman named "Tracy." I hang up. I wait five minutes before canceling the trip and select "rider no show," meaning Uber will at least pay me a small fee for my time. There are several ways to exit the mall, which is nestled back in what was once a heavily wooded area now crisscrossed with highways and on-ramps leading to the interstate. Just as I prepare to hook a left onto one of the connectors, I receive another ride request. It's Aaron again. My phone rings.

"Hello, sir. We're on the other side of the mall. The movie theater side."

"Got it," I say. "I tried to text and call."

"Uber wouldn't let me update my number until now," he says. "Dang technology."

"Dang technology," I say. "Coming around now."

By the sound of Aaron's voice, I expect to find a young white guy. Which is what I do find, although the backlighting of the mall casts Aaron and his friend in silhouettes, obscuring defining traits other than one is roughly six feet and change and lanky, the other stocky and about a head shorter. I can also see that they're both holding white Styrofoam cups and sipping from straws. Both also appear slightly disheveled, their clothes a half size too big, like maybe they hadn't bothered to take them off before bed or when they woke up.

They climb in and I learn that Aaron is the shorter one. He sits up front with me and in the brief moment of the interior lights being on, I notice his dark hair and glasses and the scraggly beard of an early twenty-something who hasn't bothered to use a straight razor enough for his beard to grow coarse and thick. He reminds me of Vincent D'Onofrio circa *Full Metal Jacket*, except his beard is more Edgar the Bug circa *Men in Black*.

"Sorry for the confusion," Aaron says. "I've been trying to change my dang number, and Uber wouldn't even recognize my Google voice."

"Geez," Aaron's friend chimes in from the back. "Step into the twenty-first century why don't ya?" Aaron's friend is a pitch-perfect, un-ironic Napoleon Dynamite. I keep waiting for a "Gosh!" or a "Freakin' idiot" to punctuate each sentence, but it never comes.

"Who's Tracy?" I ask.

"My ex," Aaron says. He lets out a sigh. I leave it at that.

"All you Uber drivers have good-smelling cars," faux-Napoleon pipes up. "Uber must've just gave you this thing, like, yesterday or something, huh?"

"Thanks," I say. "But, no, it's mine. I try to keep it clean."

"I see," Napoleon says and pauses for a beat. "Bet you don't smoke."

"Good bet," I say.

"This isn't a smoker's car," Napoleon says. "We're smokers. It's a bad habit. We'll quit when we get older, and it's not, like, something to do when we're standing outside and needing something to do to waste time."

"Sounds like a plan," I say.

"I heard most of the drivers in Knoxville own their cars," Aaron says, switching the subject. "But I heard in the big cities Uber leases the cars to drivers and takes it out of their checks. Like, how weird is that, huh? Driving around to pay for the car you're driving."

"Super meta!" Napoleon says.

"Uber meta!" I say.

"Dude!" Aaron says.

I'm still in the circular maze of the mall parking lot, my GPS not quite sure which route out is the fastest, offering multiple "similar ETAs" to choose from.

"What's the best exit?" I ask.

"You not from around here?" Napoleon says.

"I know Knoxville," I say. "But I don't know every nook and cranny. And I don't spend a lot of time at the mall."

"I see," Napoleon says, letting a beat pass. "Up to the stop sign and hang a right, then a left, then it's a straight shot to my house."

I follow his directions and maneuver beyond what woods weren't chopped down back in the mid-1980s. We hit a red light before I can make the left onto the straightaway.

"I haven't come here much since they quit calling it East Towne Mall," I say, reminiscing in my own mind of a time when my cousin lived close to this mall. Her mother and my mother would take us to the movies here, back when it was seen as "safe."

"We *still* call it East Towne," Aaron says. "Doesn't seem right to call one West Town and the other one some made-up name so people don't think the east side ain't the place to be."

"I don't disagree," I say.

"Yeah," Napoleon says. "Still got a good food court." He takes a slurp from his drink.

The light turns green and I go left, a ten-minute trip farther east, deeper into farmland and churches and a gravel turnoff here and there that leads to a trailer park hidden in the darkness of undeveloped land.

"What movie'd you two see?" I ask.

"We just came out on that side," Aaron says. "We wanted some food, and we were pricing some cards we might trade."

"Like baseball cards?" I ask.

"Heck no!" Napoleon says.

"You ever hear of Yu-Gi-Oh!?" Aaron asks.

"Can't say that I have."

"Where have you been living?" Napoleon says. "What are you, like twenty-five?"

"Thirty-one," I say.

"Do you at least know Japanese anime?" Aaron asks, going easy on me. "It's a trading card game based on *Duel Monsters*."

"I know what anime is," I say. "But that's about all I've got."

"You don't play cards?" Napoleon asks.

"I play with cards that have kings and queens on them."

"Poker," Napoleon says. "Poker's kinda fun, but you can lose too much money at poker. You can lose money in Yu-Gi-Oh! but not a lot of money. Not like a whole paycheck from Burger King."

"Stay away from casinos," Aaron says.

"I learned that lesson," I say.

I notice Aaron scrolling through his phone and discern numbers next to dollar signs. I have a tinge of regret for charging him the cancellation fee, knowing now that it was an honest mistake, the ex-girlfriend and all. I wonder if he'll question me about it, irritated that he was charged five bucks that could've gone toward a new pack of Yu-Gi-Oh! cards. He pushes the sleep button on his phone and cranes back at Napoleon. So do I. The kid's mouth is hanging half-open—no glasses, but the same Napoleon puff on top, minus the curls, plus a caterpillar mustache.

"Yo, I actually under-drafted last week," Aaron says. "I can buy us some video games."

"Under-drafted?" I ask.

"I started my first checking account on my own," Aaron says with an emphasis on *own*. "I set it up where the bank only lets me have so much a week. I was like a hundred under."

"Good you're budgeting," I say. "Smart."

"I've seen a lotta people be dumb," Aaron says.

"What video games you play?" Napoleon asks.

"I don't," I say. "Not since *Sonic the Hedgehog*, anyway."

"Freakin' A!" Napoleon says. "What do you do?"

"I read. You know, books?"

"You watch *Family Guy* at least, right?" Napoleon says.

"I watched a few seasons in college, a decade ago."

"It's called the internet," Aaron says, laughing until his shoulders bob up and down.

"I've heard of it," I say.

"The number-one game-changer for porn," Napoleon says. "Hands down the best thing the internet did."

"Um, sure," I say.

"You married or something?" Napoleon asks.

"I'm not."

"I see," Napoleon says. "So you're in the same boat as me—unless you have a girlfriend, and then you're not in the same boat as me."

"I can't even get Tinder to work on my phone," Aaron says, laughing and bobbing again. "If I could, I bet I'd be like Quagmire!"

"Giggity!" Napoleon says on cue.

"You two roommates? Go to school together?"

"We've been friends a while, huh, Dustin?" Aaron says. "Like eight, nine years. We actually met at a Yu-Gi-Oh! tournament."

"Yeah, I had to take up for this guy," Dustin (aka Napoleon) says. "He came in wearing a Power Rangers costume for no reason. I had to be like the Power Rangers are an underrated Americanized spinoff of a high-quality Japanese genre. Supreme special effects for its time."

"What color were you?" I ask.

"Green," Aaron says. "Green Ranger for life!"

Before I can reveal my ignorance about the green Power Ranger: "Tommy the Green!" Aaron yells. "Tommy does not go down. Tommy Oliver cannot be defeated in the green suit."

"Dude," Dustin says, "don't get started on the Green Ranger rules the world crap. Every guy wants to see Amy Jo in the pink suit. So many guys hit puberty on the pink suit."

"They're coming to Knoxville," Aaron says. "The real-life Tommy and Kimberly."

"I'm gonna fight Tommy," Dustin says. "I don't even know how to fight, but I'm going to fight him."

"Dude, he knows like fifteen kinds of martial arts," Aaron says. "He like invented his own kind of karate. You would get killed, like literally killed."

"Whatever," Dustin says. "It'd be all over YouTube. I'd be viral for kicking the Green Ranger right in the shin."

Aaron laughs and bobs at this, meaning he's genuinely delighted at the prospect of his friend kicking the shin of his favorite Power Ranger. "I'd be filming it," Aaron says. "My YouTube account would go nuts. I could start my own channel like PewDiePie, just not racist."

"Yeah," Dustin says. "We'd be like the second coming of Jay and

Silent Bob just cause I kicked the Green Ranger in the shin."

Dustin leans up and puts his long, skinny fingers on Aaron's shoulders and shakes him in that "you're my boy" way.

I'm less than half a mile from their turnoff, then another half mile more to their house. The highway is two-lane, street lights spread out every quarter mile, hardly a house in plain sight, most of them nestled behind a thicket of oaks and magnolias, clearings cut out into the woods and hillsides, rooftops only visible from an airplane.

"You two always lived in Knoxville?" I ask.

"Born and raised," Dustin says.

"Same," Aaron says. "I'm trying to get this one to go to Orlando with me. Been saving since last summer for Universal."

"Makes me nervous," Dustin says.

"Afraid of roller coasters?" I ask.

"I've never left Tennessee," Dustin says.

"You have to go then," I say.

"That's what I told him," Aaron says. "How're you gonna be twenty and never left Knoxville?"

"What're you afraid of?" I ask.

"People are different in big cities," Dustin says. "They eat different stuff and talk different. I wouldn't know what to order. They probably couldn't understand me."

"Think you're afraid you might like it?" I ask. "Maybe you won't want to leave."

Dustin doesn't say anything. "You'd like the rides," Aaron says, breaking the silence. "I always wanted someone to ride the rides with."

I pull off the highway, steering around sharp curves until there is a lone house set off in the dark acreage. There isn't really a gravel drive so much as a gravel lot, three cars parked out front, faint lights in a few of the windows of the one-story vinyl rancher.

"More roommates?" I ask.

"My family," Dustin says.

"I needed a place to get away," Aaron says.

"From the ex?" I ask.

"From everything," Aaron says.

"So I told him my bedroom floor was wide open," Dustin says.

"Good man you are," I say, doing my best to channel my inner nerd, although, full disclosure, I've only seen each *Star Wars* film once, as part of my civic duty.

They open the doors and the interior lights click on. I don't look much older to them, but they look like boys to me, all smiles, *Family Guy* reruns to watch, ice cream to sneak into Dustin's room, girls to discuss, or boys, or both. After my father died, my house was the hangout spot, where teenage boys would pile in because my mother was either working late or didn't mind the rooms being filled with laughter. The day after I graduated college, my mother moved out of that house and left Kingston for Knoxville, in need of distance from the memories. A couple of months later, I left for New York City, the only one of my closest high school friends not to return to our hometown and get married and eventually have a kid, or two.

I drive by that house every once in a while, when I'm in Kingston visiting those friends or my grandmother. The basketball goal has been removed, and I smile at how we all managed to fit inside those red-brick walls, every bed and couch and floor occupied, cars parked single file up the steep hill that was my driveway. It belongs to an elderly couple now, from Michigan I've heard, or somewhere up

North, and they only live there a few months out of the year, mostly during the winter. My friends and I remain in touch, play golf together at a cheap municipal course occasionally, but the laughter has been replaced by adult responsibilities, the memories replaced by new ones made with their own families, mine with new friends in new places.

For Aaron and Dustin, all that seems like a long way off. But it isn't.

"Orlando?" I say.

"Orlando," Aaron says and shuts the door.

Dustin shuts his too, and I watch as Aaron puts his arm around Dustin and squeezes his shoulder in the faint light from the windows of the house ahead. It's an "I love you." I wonder if they'll lose this feeling, if life will come between them, if Dustin's bedroom will have to hold the smiles and the late-night talks and the video games—a house to always come back to, if only to drive past and reminiscence about what might have been. ◆

Dirty
Dishes

I wrote a fictional story once about a closeted gay man living in the Bible Belt who'd dutifully accumulated a wife and two young daughters. This was 2014, back when I was living in Connecticut, working for ESPN and earning an MFA part-time. I also shared an address with my then-girlfriend, who rented a studio in Brooklyn but spent most weekends at my condo in Hartford. One Saturday night I asked her to read an early draft of the now-published story, which includes a sex scene between two teenage boys. Afterward, while I washed the dirty dishes from the dinner she'd cooked, she asked, "You're not gay, are you?"

I grinned, mostly because I was proud that my portrayal of the character had been realistic, at least to her, although, in hindsight, the question solidified the eventual deterioration of our relationship, the lack of communication—on my part—that had left her wondering if I was satisfied, not only in bed but with our life together. I promised her that I hadn't kissed a man, much less had sex with a man, nor did I have any inclination to. But I can find the muscular V of a man's torso sexy, just as she can find sexiness in the way a dress hugs a woman's backside. Of course, women can easily join in on the objectification of other women because it's our status quo, what society legitimizes in our day-to-day, from Hooters to strip clubs to the Oval Office.

In addition to the story, my girlfriend had witnessed more than one man hit on me during our stint in New York City, and she'd witnessed me laugh off every encounter, even egg the flirtation on, trading sexual innuendos with a man the same as a woman might do to procure a couple of free drinks at the bar. No matter what my Southern, Evangelical upbringing might've ingrained in me about masculinity and heterosexuality, I craved attention, no matter the gender.

I've always viewed myself as a too-skinny white guy with an average penis—according to the porn I've watched, anyway—whose physical appearance doesn't turn heads when I walk into a room, as if any of that is the actual measure of a person's worth. As a teenager I lacked self-confidence when it came to body image and the opposite sex, so much so that, after the death of my father, I latched on to a girl my sophomore year of high school and refused to let go completely until after my senior year of college. Between the ages of fifteen and thirty, I only had sexual intercourse with three women, living vicariously through my peers in college, young men I'd grown up with who'd accumulated large biceps and chiseled abs and, ostensibly, big penises; young men who ran women through a figurative revolving door, men who now have wives and children of their own and who seem satisfied and fulfilled with their nuclear lives, according to social media.

I feel silly now, having added to my list of sexual partners and arrived at the inevitable conclusion that sex doesn't fill emotional voids. I feel silly now, having met people who identify as pansexual and people who are transitioning and people in same-sex marriages and open marriages and polyamorous relationships—people who rightfully don't conflate sex with love, or love with sex, or sex with gender, or gender with sexuality, or any of those terms with toxic notions of societal roles, or relationships with religious expectations. I feel silly now because validation was what I lacked—physical validation from women because society had convinced me that my appearance and the number of women I'd slept with dictated my manhood and emotional validation from men because I'd lost my father at fifteen, the man whose hugs and "Good job, Son" were a source of immense pride.

But back then, during my formative teenage and college years and the years that I confused my bosses and colleagues in corporate America with role models, I felt alone and very conflicted about whom to look up to. My mentors at ESPN were exclusively white men, exclusively married to stay-at-home-moms. The women in the office whose husbands made lesser salaries and picked the kids up from school also seemed influenced by society's toxic masculinity, the mere act of flipping the patriarchal paradigm not enough to address corporate America's problematic water cooler.

I'm still flattered when male Uber and Lyft passengers compliment my appearance, even attempt to convince me that I don't know what I'm missing. Recently, on a humid Sunday afternoon, a man who'd had one martini too many climbed in and asked if I had a girlfriend or a wife. We'd already exchanged pleasantries, and he'd quipped about having a "Sunday Funday," to which I replied that those get me into the trouble I'm trying to stay out of.

"That's the only fun part about a Sunday," he'd laughed. I didn't know right away how inebriated the man was, or that he liked men, only that he was a black man with a neat, close-cut fade and a thin mustache. As is often the case with early-afternoon drinkers, he maintained his composure for the first few minutes of the ride before his slight slur clued me in to the situation—that and when he said, "You're cute," and then asked, "Can I touch your face?"

It's a tricky situation for a straight white man: a drunk black man hitting on you from your backseat. I understand that the seemingly obvious response should be "Thanks, but I'm not interested." Leave it at that. (That didn't work, which we'll get to.) But more than a few straight men I know would have pulled over and threatened the man if he didn't get out. Maybe even pulled him out of the car by force. I'm not asking for a pat on the back for being accepting, but I am asking that we not ignore the toxically masculine reactions that are perpetuated by religion and politics and pop culture. Let's be honest: If I would've agreed to his touching my face, then this becomes an entirely different story, doesn't it?

Instead, the man realized that we'd gone ten minutes down the interstate in the wrong direction. He initially blamed me until he checked the data he'd entered into the app, an address for a massage parlor where he worked on the complete other side of town. I didn't particularly care where he was going, or how many miles it might take to get there, only that he acknowledged the awkwardness of the dynamic when I said, "I'm not gay."

"I can change your mind," he said. "I have men and women wanting me to be more than just their masseur. All my clients feel special."

I asked what kind of music he liked, and he simply said, "Bey," so I cued up some Beyoncé, and then he asked what kind of music I liked.

"All kinds," I said.

"That ain't the vibe you give off," he said. "Seems like you only like one kind."

The implication was clear, and I mostly wanted the ride to be over, just as I imagine a Hooters' waitress would want a table of ogling men to close out their tabs. (Or maybe they're worth the added annoyance for the tip.)

"Who doesn't know what kind of music they like?" he insisted.

"Is this an analogy?" I asked.

"No, bitch, it's a question. Are you not grown enough to think for yourself?"

I didn't owe him an answer, any more than I needed to pull over. The disappointment, at least for me, was in the fact that we hadn't left any room for compromise or for understanding. The assumption is that I'm not open to loving a man, and I'm not certain that assumption isn't wrong, that life hasn't ingrained in me that love and sexual desires are conflated, to the point that I'd never love a man because I couldn't be sexually intimate with him.

The rest of the trip I played a Beyoncé radio station, and he shimmied and shook, tapping my shoulder occasionally to ask again if he could touch my face, before facetiously pulling his hand away: "Wouldn't want you to get all salty."

"I'm Quentin," he said finally, revealing his name instead of the Q he'd entered in the app. "You're tense. You just need a night to let me rub that out."

I laughed at "Quentin," didn't egg him on, although he did ask if I wanted to come inside. For a brief moment, I wondered, *What if?*

• • •

MAN IN THE (REARVIEW) MIRROR

Since returning to the South, I've done my best to devote more time to my mother and my grandmother, a weekend once or twice a month on the lake in Kingston, Tennessee. My mother does more of the cooking these days, although my grandmother still fries the okra and the chicken, still fixes the potato salad. The minute stomachs are full, I start stacking the empty plates and try to wash the dirty dishes before either woman can get to them. My grandmother always makes a point to comment on a young man like me doing such a thing without being told, the implication being that a young man like me ought to want to sit with the men who remain in my life, crossing our legs and discussing the pitiful state of the Union and bygone years when America made sense.

My mother sends me text messages afterward, saying how responsible I am, how no other man she knows does the things I do, as if washing dirty dishes is somehow beneath me. I don't tell either of them that I'd do anything to not have to sit on the porch and listen to the men, afraid I might say something that can't be undone.

I let hot water and suds cascade over my hands until they're wrinkled, until the dishes are done and the men have had enough to eat and drink and are ready for bed, leaving the porch for me and my granny. I wash them so that I don't have to explain why it is that I don't believe tasks like washing dishes are intended for women, or why it is that I wish I could go back to 2014 and tell that woman I used to wash dirty dishes for all that I didn't know how to say. ◆

Black Lives Matter

PART 1

One of the things that distinguishes Americans from other people is that no other people has ever been so deeply involved in the lives of black men, and vice versa. This fact faced, with all its implications, it can be seen that the history of the American Negro problem is not merely shameful, it is also something of an achievement. For even when the worst has been said, it must also be added that the perpetual challenge posed by this problem was always, somehow, perpetually met. It is precisely this black-white experience which may prove of indispensable value to us in the world we face today. This world is white no longer, and it will never be white again.

—JAMES BALDWIN, "Stranger in the Village," 1953

I once picked up a blind man of Native American descent. He was certain that I had taken advantage of his inability to see by going the scenic route to raise the fare a few bucks. In hindsight, the trip confirms for me that blind trust is a fragile notion between a man with

27tory

sight and a man without—same as it is between a white man and a man whose skin is varying shades darker than mine; or a man who does not love as I love, in the heterosexual sense; or a man who was not raised as I was raised, in the Evangelical sense; not to mention between myself and a woman, much less a woman who checks off any of those "other" boxes.

Once that blind man of Native American descent felt slighted for an existence he did not choose, then his trust toward me, in its textbook definition, was erased. All that could potentially be reached between us was reconciliation. But that blind man and I did not get the chance to reconcile. I wonder still if our encounter lodged in his subconscious, bolstering his belief that the majority will never welcome him fully because of his inability to see, and because of the majority's ability to see that his skin already places him in the minority.

So, as if to offer an opportunity to correct my previous over-generalization, the universe paired me with another blind man, who was white and in his early thirties, same as I. In a small market like Knoxville, Tennessee, you often encounter repeat customers, so I had actually given him a ride before, although it was only a matter of minutes, time enough for the pleasantries. I recognized the neighborhood, more of a long street really, lined with nondescript, free-standing condos, all of them connected to one-car garages and paved carports, each lit by a fluorescent floodlight. It was pitch black when I arrived, a fact that is perhaps useless to mention, considering darkness is the blind man's perpetual state of being.

As I was pulling in, "Andy" walked out, eyes closed, and I wondered if he'd always been blind. He was wearing a plain white T-shirt and blue jeans and dirty white tennis shoes. His hair was as black as the jacket he had on, maybe Members Only. He felt around with his metal stick until he reached my back door, and I watched over my shoulder as he retracted the stick and felt his way in. He'd sat in the front on our previous trip. I considered whether he chose based on the first door he'd reached, or if he had, like many people, decided that Uber was a cab service now, and that I was merely his chauffeur.

"Just to Steak 'n Shake and back," he said.

Before I could respond, Andy spoke into his phone, what I assumed to be a voice text. It was small talk mostly, although I was surprised to hear that Andy had purchased a PlayStation 4. "The voice command function was sorely lacking," he told the person he was texting, "so I took it back. They said they don't usually do returns, but in this case they'd make an exception—damn right they'd make an exception."

I'd failed to speed through a yellow light, so we were left idling for a while at an intersection near the interstate. I'd been playing music but turned it down when Andy commenced screaming into his phone. It was just a faint white noise now, but Andy's ears located it: "Where is that awful music coming from?" I turned the volume to zero.

"Long light," I said.

"Always is," he said.

I wasn't sure if he meant this particular traffic light, or if he was implying I'd purposefully gotten caught by it. I pushed the thought aside. The light turned green, and Andy kept dictating to his phone, his "sentence period, sentence period" routine. I navigated the interstate for a few mile markers, a couple of exits, until we took the off-ramp toward Steak 'n Shake. I'd assumed we were going through the drive-thru but realized this Steak 'n Shake didn't have one. I parked near the door.

"Are we here?" Andy asked.

"We are," I said.

"You're going to have to help me."

I certainly didn't mind, but leading a strange blind man into a restaurant full of strangers hadn't been something I'd bargained for when I signed up to be an Uber driver.

"Come around to my side," Andy instructed.

I took direction and climbed out of the car. When I reached him, he asked for my left arm. I put a crook in it, as though Andy and I were preparing to walk down the aisle. He gently straightened it and clasped my bicep. We shuffled along.

"Step up ahead," I said as we approached the sidewalk. "Now," I said, and Andy raised his foot a few inches higher until it connected with the concrete. I pushed open the door with my free hand, and we awkwardly walked through, shoulder to shoulder, only to be in a tiny vestibule with another door to conquer. We repeated the push-shuffle routine and were enveloped by the savory sweet scent of grease mixed with butter. My mouth watered from the saltiness. Eyes were on us and my face flushed, this blind man I barely knew holding my arm for support. I didn't turn to address the crowd, instead keeping my eyes on the young blonde at the cash register, who looked at Andy and then at me, recognition in her eyes, a smile of pity more than kindness.

"We're at the counter," I said. Andy let loose of my bicep and stretched both arms out until his hands rested on the credit card machine. "Pick up for Andy," he said. "Two hamburgers, two large fries, two large Cokes."

"Coming right up, sir," she chirped. She had on a red visor and a red apron, both emblazoned with "Steak 'n Shake" in letters as white as her smile. She disappeared into the steam and silvery light of the industrial kitchen, reemerging with two Styrofoam cups bigger around than my biceps and a white paper bag darkened by grease in spots. The receipt was stapled to the bag, and she ripped it free, punching numbers into her computer screen before calling out the final tally.

"Hold it right there, honey," Andy said, lolling his head with attitude. "Read off what's on those burgers."

She shifted her green eyes at me, raising her brows. She stretched the receipt taught between both hands and ticked off some specific type of mayo, two different types of cheeses, light on mustard, heavy on ketchup. "That all?" she asked.

"Fries?" Andy asked.

"Curly?" the girl said, as if she was now questioning everything printed in black and white on the receipt.

"That'll do," he said. Andy ran his hands until they hit the slit in the credit card reader.

"It's a chip," the girl said.

I cradled Andy's hand and helped him push the card into the slot. "You'll have to sign for me." I didn't even know his last name, so I scribbled "Andy Something" with the stylus pen. I gathered that the return trip from the register to my car would be more daunting: Andy holding my bicep in one hand and the giant-size Coke in the other; me a bag filled with the weight of two half-pound burgers in one hand, a giant-size Coke in the other, all while leading a blind man.

"Have a wonderful night," the waitress said as we inched away, ice sloshing to mark time with our steps.

Andy halted. "We should have straws," he announced to anyone listening.

"I have them," I said. "They didn't forget."

"You have to watch them," Andy said.

We were back in the car and on the road without casualty. That warm feeling of having done a good deed welled up inside of me, and I figured that a rapport had surely been created between us, although it struck me then that this was simply a night in the life for Andy.

"You ever have trouble getting a driver to do that," I asked, glancing up in the rearview. Andy's head had been tilted at the window, perhaps toward the sound of cars rushing by on the interstate. He turned in the direction of my voice.

"What?" he asked, oblivious.

"Do all drivers agree to help you?"

"All of them," he said. "Some are better than others. I'd say no one wants me to give them a bad rating or contact Uber."

"I drove a blind man once," I said, "and he accused me of taking him the long way."

"Common," Andy said. "You learn early not to trust."

"If you don't mind me asking, have you always been blind?"

"Always."

"Again, you don't have to answer, but I'm curious. What happened?"

"Retinopathy of prematurity mixed with a little oxygen toxicity," Andy said. "In layman's terms: I was born extremely premature. They pumped so much oxygen into my incubator that my retinas detached."

"God," I said.

"He had something to do with it," he said.

I hadn't been able to place the tune, nor had I been focused on it, but I realized now that Andy had been faintly humming "What a Friend We Have in Jesus" while holding my arm as we entered the Steak 'n Shake, occasionally mouthing the words.

"Were there any repercussions?" I asked.

"Only my sight," he said.

"I guess I meant for the doctors."

Andy scoffed. "It was blind or die. My parents picked the former."

Maybe I was hearing what I wanted—the shame of the able-bodied white man in me—but there was a curtness to Andy's answers, bordering on resentfulness, as if the recitation of his disability over all these years had hardened him, confirmed that he was doomed to live in the margins. I imagine in some ways he wasn't wrong. The man couldn't change the fact that he was blind, nor could he change the realities and generalities his blindness had imposed on him.

"Sorry to pry," I said. "I just find it genuinely fascinating, especially in times like these."

"What do you mean?" Andy asked.

He had seemed beyond offending, almost defiant in that he wouldn't let his lack of sight render him lesser. But this was that pivotal moment, when I would have to prove that I wasn't merely marveling at the capabilities of an invalid. "I just mean your inability to see color," I said, "what with all the racial upheaval this year—Dallas, Milwaukee, Charlotte."

"Don't even get me started on that Black Lives Matter crap," Andy said, rocking up in his seat. "Just a bunch of people wanting attention. Let me tell you, their ancestors would be doing backflips in their graves if they saw the opportunities black people had today. Doing backflips."

To steal a line from the author and essayist Ta-Nehisi Coates, I was shocked at my own shock. Which rendered me mute for a stretch and allowed Andy to continue his rant about a pigment he couldn't actually see. My attention faded in and faded out, reminded of the final few passages from the essay "Notes of a Native Son" by Coates's predecessor, the late author and essayist James Baldwin: "[B]lackness and whiteness did not matter; to believe that they did was to acquiesce in one's own destruction. Hatred, which could destroy so much, never failed to destroy the man who hated and this was an immutable law."

Then I heard Andy say, "If the damned media wouldn't have given black people a voice, they would've disappeared, no attention, which is all they want."

"Guess we could say the same about Donald Trump."

Andy paused. I knew what I was doing, and I'm sure he did too. I knew his kind, blind or not. I've sat on their couches and felt their guns underneath the cushions, ready for the black and brown enemies they've heard about on TV. I've seen the ceramic Mammy cookie jars they collect as antiques, as if the symbolic racism of the Confederate South should be set inside a glass case as proof of history, of a simpler time, appreciated rather than abhorred.

"Donald Trump was saying what we all wanted to say," Andy said. "We are paying for the immorality and the criminality of people who don't belong in this country. If we need to kill as a means to protect our homeland, then we should kill. Illegals and Islam have no place here."

"I'd say Hitler would've agreed."

"Hitler was a visionary in many ways," Andy said. "Have you read *Mein Kampf*?"

"I have," I said, wondering if anything might be lost in translation to Braille. "I'm a writer. I believe in the power of words and persuasion. I'm also aware of the slippery slope that is ideology and that is propaganda."

"Hitler's radicalism simply wasn't checked," Andy said, "and we have the ability to do that in this country."

"The line between fascism and good intentions can become so thin you can hardly see it," I said. "But I hope you're right."

"Are you from around here?" Andy asked.

"I am," I said.

"Then you know the Confederate flag is part of our history," he said. "Why are we being asked to erase it? Why are we being asked to erase Jesus from our schools?"

"The swastika was part of history too," I said. "Same as Muhammad."

"Look," Andy said, "Obama wasn't a bad president, if he's who you're sad about. He was a good man. But he was too meek and too mild—he wasn't going to protect us against a foreign enemy or uphold our moral values."

"Who's us?" I said.

"The American people," Andy said.

"Black Lives Matter people?" I said more than asked. I told Andy that Barack Obama walked a tightrope for eight years, barely losing his balance, while the majority in his own country hurled everything at him but the kitchen sink. A majority, mind you, of which he is a part, raised by his white mother and grandparents.

"The American people have already spoken," Andy said. "But you can still have your opinions. Isn't this country beautiful?"

"Isn't it though?" I said. "We shall see what we shall see."

That was our agree to disagree. Andy and I had a few more miles left to go in relative silence, and I recounted Ta-Nehisi Coates's cover story in *The Atlantic*, "My President Was Black," published after Trump was elected. Coates chronicled the history Obama defied and the future it arguably leads us to face. Coates has been held to a lofty standard, one he embraces and explicitly tries to attain, a standard of explicating the condition of the black American in the same exacting-yet-nuanced detail as Baldwin. It's a task akin to asking LeBron James to replicate the impact Michael Jordan had not only on the NBA but also on an American culture that had yet to witness a black man become a global corporate brand. Jordan's talent found itself in the middle of evolution and subsequent revolution, albeit in a pro sports league and not politics. Rarely has a white man been asked to define and defend his culture, or truly thought it necessary to provide nuance to the inherent power his words contain. Meanwhile, Coates finds himself in an unenviable sociopolitical era, when revolution seems halfhearted, when humanity, or maybe just white America, seems to be just fine with resting on its laurels.

As for Baldwin, he wrote in a time when black and white were organized, unafraid to break laws to prove the injustice and inequality of those laws. Now, a few Facebook friends is all we're willing to lose in the name of equality, not our livelihoods or our individual freedoms. I have been guilty of hiding behind screens, as well as unduly negating Coates's impact, mostly out of my own white fear that he is right, and I am the problem, no need for any gray area.

So perhaps I should alter my sports analogy to give Coates his due—perhaps he is the literary scene's Allen Iverson, the cornrows and tats and "talkin' bout practice" to Jordan's seemingly harmless bald head and wagging tongue, a work ethic honed by the likes of black whisperer Dean Smith at North Carolina, as opposed to Georgetown's John Thompson, a black man himself who plucked Iverson from the streets, not the suburbs. There are those who say Coates has denigrated President Obama unjustly, that Coates's insistence on Obama's playing both sides—both black and white—is a shortsighted assessment of a president who must play the game of the system to produce results. They say that President Obama's being above the role of the "angry black man" is precisely the reason he has risen to such great heights.

However, I wonder if rising above doesn't unintentionally beget looking down. I wonder if turning a blind eye is worse than calling it like you see it. From where I'm sitting, I can see that the natural rebuttal, for a white man at least, would be to tick off the number of schools and streets dedicated to Martin Luther King Jr., not to Malcolm X. But to begrudge Coates, who was born and raised in Baltimore the son of a former Black Panther, for stating the obvious, for reminding us that black men remain at a disadvantage and that overtly racist men like Andy (blind or not) do in fact still exist, would be no different than to begrudge Andy for wishing he could see a sunrise and a sunset just once in his life.

Black male writers like Coates are not in the business of playing games, of passing the ball, for which they have no more patience. Coates and his contemporaries—like Kiese Laymon, who escaped the racism of his native Mississippi before returning to be a professor at Ole Miss—have watched their grandparents and their parents, many of them college educated, kowtow to the white man in the hope of getting a word in edgewise. But to what end? Coates and Laymon ask this question unequivocally. Why give voice to the oppressor, whose nature is to oppress, or at the least to not lose his place in the pecking order?

Every time I read the work of Coates and Laymon, I wonder if I'm the white folk they are talking about. I know that I am, but I do not want to be. I look deep inside myself and entertain the notion that I am racist, inherently. I often grow angry at them because they are right. And I am wrong. And there is no other explanation. While I was at ESPN as a senior editor, Laymon enacted a bit of a coup by finding his way into the pages of *ESPN The Magazine*, writing an essay, "How They Do in Oxford," about the remains of the Confederacy at Ole Miss, a place where young black men don pads and helmets in the shadow of Dixie, where rich white folk tailgate heavily and drink profusely, always raising a glass to the fictional plantation owner, Colonel Reb, as if the land of cotton should not in fact be forgotten.

I call it a coup because the essay went to press under the same editor-in-chief who had once told me that black quarterbacks were a nonissue, that I was living in the mind-set of the backward South whence I came. (I left the company before Colin Kaepernick began taking a knee for the national anthem, and that editor-in-chief has since departed to run a gambling site.) That same editor-in-chief, a white man, also once told a room of us at the magazine that an entire issue on "race in sports" sounded about as interesting as a book report. I often wonder if that editor was simply biding his time until The Undefeated website was launched, a site affiliated with the ESPN mothership but allowed to orbit in DC, far from the gated, predominantly white campus in Bristol, Connecticut. The

Undefeated refers to itself as "the premier platform for exploring the intersections of race, sports and culture." I would argue, however, that it is the premier platform for ESPN to siphon off its coverage of the racially controversial, so as to not interfere with the company's scores and highlights, to keep from annoying the white men it serves with the struggles of the black men it covers, as if the lives of those black men are simply fantasy points, lives to be measured on mobile or on desktop, with page views and ad revenues and stock prices.

Coates and Laymon, to the white man's chagrin, remind us that this game we play has legitimate consequences. President Obama belonged where no black man had before, but his margin for error was nonexistent. He might well have been an aberration as opposed to a human being, a man who transcended color in a way so unprecedented that the very black men he empowered became saddled with an even heavier burden, the burden of lifting a race while the white world continues to ignore the systemic deck that has been stacked against it.

When we arrived at Andy's condo, he expected me to help him carry the Steak 'n Shake inside. I obliged, and he warned me that there was a dog that might approach me but wasn't vicious. He used his metal stick instead of holding my arm. I registered the implication now of the two gigantic drinks, although not until we crossed the threshold did I consider that a woman would be inside. The dog, a greyhound, approached, and I stood still.

"She's only smelling him," the woman said, referring to the greyhound.

I'd entered into a narrow hallway that ended at the living room, where the woman sat on a couch, which was positioned less than two feet from a flat-screen TV, video game consoles and DVDs strewn about her. By her comment about the dog, I surmised that she could see, although her glasses must've been a half-inch thick. She didn't move off the couch. I continued down the hall, stains of varying color dotting the off-white carpet. I reached the kitchen, which was equally disheveled, dishes stacked everywhere because the sink was already piled too high. Andy told me to set the food and the drink on the table, on a space that he'd cleared of newspapers and magazines. I wondered if they were in Braille or if the woman on the couch with the thick glasses read them to him.

"Thanks," Andy said once he'd heard the Steak 'n Shake hit the table. The woman with the thick glasses finally got up, and I retreated to the door.

I walked out into the chilly December night and saw my breath. I'd left the car running to stay warm. I considered how we might address the hate in our hearts, the hate that Baldwin so poignantly defines, the hate that Coates and Laymon exorcise to remind us of our prejudices. But what of Andy, the man who cannot see the skin he despises? I understood now that the hate Baldwin speaks of can only be found in the mirror, that even a blind man can see inside himself, that closing our eyes might, in fact, be the only way to see. ◆

The Women
at the Country Club

On a Thursday around midnight, I received a ride request from "Buffy." That isn't the woman's real name, but I choose it in keeping with the white, upper-class stereotype of her real name. I pulled into the circle drive of a country club to find Buffy and two other fifty-something women wobbling aimlessly on the sidewalk. They were tipsy and giggling, making a show of merely getting into my car.

"We need to see your Uber credentials," one of the women said in a low, serious tone, mimicking a police officer. She climbed up front with me and had yet to shut the door, leaving the overhead light on. She squinted at me, and I squinted back.

"You look like my teenage son!" she shouted, closing the door. We were illuminated by the fluorescent blues and greens off the dash.

"Why, he's barely old enough to drive!" Buffy squealed, which morphed into a high-pitched guffaw. The other two women joined in. A chorus of *ha-ha-ha*'s.

It shouldn't bother me that I look young, that I often feel like a thirty-one-year-old trapped inside a twenty-five-year-old exterior (more like twenty-two on days when I actually shave). But it does bother me. I think the insecurity stems from having spent my life searching for approval from adults, being that I lost my father at fifteen. There is also a perceived stigma—especially below the Mason-Dixon Line and in Small Town USA—that comes with being unmarried and childless post-thirty, as though those are necessary rites of passage into proper adulthood. I've spent much of my adult life constantly fighting to transcend Southern stereotypes, to have my opinions heard and my ideas respected, a respect that tends to come with either titles on your résumé or a ring on your finger. Yet now that I actually have the former and have avoided the latter, I'm still sized up on first glance as a college kid driving people around for beer money.

I don't necessarily mind the jokes. But to open the conversation with a judgment based solely on my appearance, no matter how innocuous, doesn't create much of a rapport with me. It's really no different than my blurting out, "God, you're fat!" the minute we meet.

So, admittedly, my first impression of these passengers was clouded unfairly with negative connotations. Those women might as well have been wearing pearl earrings and toting Chanel handbags to match their Louboutins. Maybe they were. But I didn't particularly care to give them anymore thought than they had me. They were ostensibly rich, as well as being older women, and I was ostensibly middle class, as well as being a younger man. And we were all as white as their collars. That was about all the nuance any of us had cared to consider.

When I read their destination aloud to confirm, Buffy interrupted: "No, no, no. Three stops. I'm last."

"Alright," I said. "Does anyone want to give me the address?"

"Just turn left, honey," the woman up front said, patting my shoulder. "We'll tell you how to get there."

"Could I at least get the name of the road?" I asked, not in the mood for passenger-seat driving. After a beat, once she'd registered my slight irritation, the woman whose teenage son I resemble gave me the name of her road. "I know it," I said. I'd dropped off a gas station attendant at that road earlier, after his shift had ended at 10. I was surprised, having seen the gas station attendant's modest, one-story house, that this woman and her pearls resided on the same street.

"Ladies, let's keep the night alive," Buffy crooned with Southern gentility. "We should have this boy take us to that place. The one the cute bartender at the club told us about."

Buffy was the tipsiest, and the two other women recalled the name of the bar right away. The club was on the complete opposite side of town, and the two women quickly dismissed the idea, reminding Buffy that their night should've ended an hour ago.

"It would've been fun, though, wouldn't it?" Buffy said. "I bet this young man has been there. Haven't you, Son?"

"I drop a lot of people off there," I said.

"Think we'd fit in?" she asked.

"I'm not sure," I said.

"Are you saying we're too old?" Buffy playfully retorted.

"I'm saying it tends to be a gay crowd on Thursday night. Are you gay?"

"Oh, goodness gracious," Buffy said. "We're not *gay*. You're not *gay*, are you? You don't sound gay."

"How does gay sound?"

Buffy burst out a *ha-ha-ha*, but the other women didn't join in.

"I've had more men tell me I'm cute than women," I said. "Maybe the Lord's giving me a hint."

"Oh, goodness," Buffy said. "You're a hoot."

"I try," I said.

"So what's your name again?" Buffy asked.

"LaRue," I said.

"You're pulling our legs," Buffy snorted and tapped my shoulder from the backseat. "You just made that up."

"No. No I didn't."

"Who would name their child *LaRue*?" Buffy chirped.

I let the question settle into the silence. Just like people questioning my age, questioning my lack of a wife and a child, I've grown exhausted with the fascination over my name, a fascination that people chalk up to uniqueness, yet I contend the fascination is predicated on the very fact that most white men from small-town Tennessee aren't named anything unique. I've grown exhausted with people saying, "That's *really* your name, like, your *real* name?" as if I concocted an alternate identity to be an Uber driver. I've become so exhausted with the whole song and dance that I didn't have the energy to give Buffy the benefit of the doubt.

I took a left onto the road where the woman in the front seat lived. There was eventually a fork. She was headed in the opposite direction of the gas station attendant's house, up a steep, curvy hill that overlooked the less-expensive neighborhood. I continued to climb, and when I rounded a curve near the top, I saw a concrete wall lit by a spotlight, a neighborhood moniker etched into the stone. It's long been a stereotypical signifier to me, a sort of DO NOT ENTER sign for those who can't afford multistory homes and in-ground pools and enough vehicles to fill a three-car garage.

"That's just offensive," I said finally. "You know you're implying that my parents made some kind of mistake in picking my name?"

Buffy fumbled: "What? No, no, no. Not at all. That's not us at all. We would never mean to insult you."

I pulled into the driveway of the woman up front, who was side-eyeing me, seemingly glad to be getting out of the car at this juncture. Her house was two stories and brick and had a two-car garage, not three. I put the car in park, and we idled, the woman up front hesitant to move before there was a resolution.

"But who's heard of a name like that?" Buffy asked. "What'd you expect? For heaven's sake, my name's Buffy!"

"And what does that prove?" I asked. "That's like saying I should've gone ahead and asked how the bridge and snifter of brandy was back at the country club. Or how many rounds of golf you got in."

That's a gross generalization that I must unlearn, a stereotype I've begun to overcome as I've dropped off more and more people in neighborhoods like this, where one multistory brick house is nearly impossible to discern from the next—other than the meticulousness of the landscaping and cost of the mailbox. But why should I not say what's on my mind, in this era of saying what's really on our minds? In this era of speech being free to everyone? Why should I reserve my assumptions when Buffy doesn't offer me the same unassuming courtesy? When she asks her questions out of disbelief rather than curiosity?

"Well, you're not far off!" Buffy said and *ha-ha-ha*'d.

I turned to the woman up front. She put her hand on my shoulder and patted it, as she might do to her own teenage son, the one who looks like me. I knew I had two more stops to make with these two other women, and I knew they were fine with living up to a stereotype, especially one that comes with privilege. Stereotypes are funny that way. They can feel as soft and comforting as a mink coat, but also as bulletproof as a flak jacket, when they come with multistory houses and in-ground pools and three-car garages and snifters of Rémy Martin.

I wondered if I even had a battle worth fighting, seeing as how my only complaints were growing up in a one-story house with an aboveground pool that collapsed and no garage at all.

"Let's just start all over," Buffy and the woman in the backseat pleaded. "We're sorry. Let's just start again. We didn't know you'd be so sensitive."

I did what many people who suffer actual prejudice do: I waved the white flag. Satisfied that we'd reconciled sufficiently, the woman up front said good-bye to her friends and told them she'd call in the morning. They would have to figure out how to retrieve the cars they'd left at the country club.

As I headed out of the neighborhood and back down the steep, curvy hill, the woman next to Buffy asked, "So what's your story, honey? Start at the beginning."

We only had eight minutes or so, along winding roads through well-to-do neighborhoods. I told them I'd been named for my father, that he'd been given a nickname at a very young age, "Boots," which had stuck, so much so that it became his only name in Kingston, the small town where he'd been part-owner of the local newspaper and where I was raised. I told them about graduating from the University of Tennessee and leaving for New York City, about ESPN, and about leaving a steady paycheck to pursue my own writing, to travel, to figure out how I'd let eight years pass without addressing the sadness that had lingered.

"Are you an only child?" Buffy asked. "You sound like an only child."

I didn't ask what an only child sounds like. I calmly told Buffy that my family dynamic was as unique as my name, that my biological father was fifty-nine when I was born and that I have half-siblings from my father's first marriage who are more than twice my age.

"Oh, goodness," Buffy said. "How odd."

The other woman must've been sobering up, or had finally recognized the tension that rose and fell with each of my exchanges with Buffy. "Is your father still alive?" she asked.

I told the story I've already told many times to my passengers, the one about my father tripping on the sidewalk after leaving my high school basketball game and smacking his head on the concrete. How his seventy-four-year-old brain hemorrhaged and he went into a coma, passing away a week later.

"I'm so sorry to hear that," Buffy said, without qualification.

"So what about you two—what are your stories?" I asked in my most upbeat tone, the awkwardness starting to dissipate.

"Oh, my!" Buffy exclaimed. "Goodness." I heard her pat the hand of the other woman. "We're just not that interesting."

"Everybody's got a story," I said. "There's happiness and sadness and hope in all our stories."

"You don't know sadness," the other woman said in a faraway voice. I glanced up in the rearview and could see the flash of her almond eyes in the haze of moonlight. She was a brunette, slender face, slight wrinkles belying the former smoothness of her youth. Her statement was unsettlingly bold, her voice so steady that I wasn't even sure if she was speaking to me or to Buffy, as though the "you" were royal, as if she were telling that to the world.

"I lost my father at fifteen," I said. "I'm not sure I can say I feel sad so much as disappointed. I would've liked to meet him as an adult. You know?"

"I do know," the woman said, snapping out of her trance. "I lost my mother at twenty-one, cancer."

It was the quietest Buffy had been, as if she were being reverent to our losses. Or perhaps Buffy was protecting herself, unwilling to let her own losses escape into my car, where she'd have to relive them, letting bad memories prey on her like shadows in the light of the moon.

"You never know who you might've been," I said. "You can't trace the what-ifs, cause there's no end. I wonder sometimes if I would've even left Tennessee."

"You're right," the other woman said. "What a parent means is indefinable, until they're gone. And still you don't know what might've been."

I maneuvered passed another concrete headstone with a made-up neighborhood name etched into it. The woman lived atop a steep driveway, and she pleaded that I not go to the trouble of climbing it, that she didn't mind walking up so I wouldn't have to deal with the hassle of backing down. Before I could insist, Buffy interjected: "If I can get an SUV down this thing, then he can get this tiny car down." I revved the engine and sped up to the paved carport; the other woman opened the door, thanking me for the conversation and the ride.

With the interior lights on, I glanced back to see the other woman hand Buffy a to-go coffee cup with a black lid. "This is almost full!" Buffy said. "You are a lightweight!" They'd been sipping on some kind of alcohol, passing it back and forth. The woman was petite, wearing a thin, black long-sleeve sweater with white denim jeans. She still had a figure, hips a smidge wider than her waist. I also stole a glimpse of Buffy before the other woman closed the door: long wispy hair, graying with black roots. She was wearing a loose-fitting navy blouse, denim jeans that weren't nearly as skinny as her friend's.

The woman shut the door, and Buffy lurched forward to wave, her fingers wagging beside my head. "She's such a beautiful woman," Buffy said as I inched down the driveway in reverse. "She's a widow, like me."

Buffy slurped the unknown liquid from the to-go cup. I didn't know how to approach the revelation other than to say, "I hate you lost your husband," as we twisted through more back roads to another concrete sign lit by a spotlight.

"Old age," Buffy said. "Just old age."

"Still, I'm sorry," I said. "What about your friend?"

"He was a good man," she said, "active in the community." Buffy told me the other woman's husband had been the "right-hand man" to the owner of a popular chain of restaurants.

"If you don't mind me asking," I said, "how'd he die?"

Buffy hiccupped. She slurped. "By his own hand," she said.

We rode for a few minutes without making a sound. I did not know this sadness. I did not know if this woman's husband had taken his own life last year or last week. I did not know if these women were one another's only comfort, a trio of widows who were left with large life insurance payouts and big, empty houses. I knew loneliness, but I did not know this kind of loss.

"Money troubles," Buffy said, unprompted. She took a slurp.

"I thought you said he was the right-hand man?"

"He had his own vices," Buffy said.

I didn't pry anymore.

"Her daughter is married to a good young man. A lawyer. They have a little girl, and they just found out they're expecting another." I could sense Buffy's smile, even if I couldn't see it. "He would be so happy."

I did not know this happiness, either, the sharing of a life, the creating of new ones. There was an optimism in Buffy that I now admired, and I wondered if the suffering through, no matter the number of cars in your garage, is the rite of passage.

"Her other daughter's a lesbian," Buffy blurted out. "He wouldn't know what to think if he were here: two grandkids and a gay daughter!" Buffy *ha-ha-ha*'d and patted her own knee. "He'd love 'em all to pieces. He would."

Some nights I drive for the purity of the task—the concentration necessary to hold a conversation and maneuver the road; the hand-eye-foot coordination necessary to operate an automobile; and the storytelling, stories that only the passenger and I may ever hear in exactly the same way.

Some nights I just enjoy being in the company of others, the visceral connection that a digital community cannot replicate. And on some nights, like this one, I fear I'm cheapening the purity of the thing by even writing this story, by possibly breaking the trust of people who tell me things in assumed confidence, never the wiser that I will relate our moment to the world.

Within humanity there is an innate trust that I'd still like to believe in, one that reminds us of our commonality, an unassuming nature that reinforces Alexander Pope: "To err is human." I don't take these lives lightly, and I can't ignore that Buffy would probably have never said what she said to me if not for the liquid in the cup. And certainly not if she were told her words would be written for the world to read. Would any of us?

I have to admit to you that Buffy's house was the biggest of the three, a circle drive all its own, two stories and a garage for three cars. It was a house bigger than I've ever lived in or probably ever will. But what does that matter, truly, when both our houses sit empty, our loneliness not equated to any square footage or dollar amount?

Buffy must've dozed off because I didn't hear any movement when I shifted to park. "We're here," I said. There was rustling and fishing through her purse. A twenty-dollar bill appeared next to me on the console.

"Too much," I said, sliding it back.

"I want to," Buffy said, "all those stops you had to make."

"Thank you," I said. "Appreciate it."

Buffy took her cup and her purse and shut the door. She didn't say good-bye. We were all alone now, in our respective places—me and Buffy and Buffy's two friends.

I stretched the twenty taut and remembered how my mother would give me one in high school after my father had died, how I'd stretch it into lunch money, plus a few McDonald's value meals over the course of a week. I was back there, stretching a twenty, while Buffy and her friends tossed them around. Although I figure they'd probably spend a lot of twenties to get their old lives back, to hear the sound of a welcome voice in those big, empty houses. ◆

Black Lives
Matter

PART 2

When I began this trilogy, Donald Trump had yet to be inaugurated. He had yet to place a temporary ban on immigrants and refugees from seven Muslim-majority countries. He had yet to call Rep. John Lewis, a black Civil Rights leader, "all talk" and "no action."

As a writer, it is dangerous to comment in real time, to let the outside world dictate the path of your story. It is dangerous because, no matter what book you believe in, or if you believe in any book at all, there are external forces that we, as humans, can simply not control, a narrative that is impossible to predict. So while I am ashamed that President Trump is considering a border wall, that he has resoundingly denounced diplomacy by insulting entire ethnicities, and that he ridiculed a preeminent Civil Rights activist, I am also glad (in that narcissistic way) that he has legitimized these essays.

Part of me, as a white man, worried that I did not have the right to speak on the matter of black lives—or on any non-white lives, for that matter. But black lives do, in fact, matter. And perhaps the interpretation of that phrase is why the movement has unsettled white America. White America was much more comfortable when the possibility of a black man in the White House seemed an impossibility. White America was much more comfortable when their teenaged offspring didn't openly idolize black rappers, when Beyoncé wasn't pop culture's ultimate icon. White America was much more comfortable before the black athletes they pay to watch play a game demanded to be more than a jersey and a pair of shoes, demanded to be human. White America was much more comfortable when their coworkers could be multiracial but the boss man was reliably white.

I am Southern and always will be. The South is where I was born and where I was raised and where I was educated. It is my birthright. But I do not have to sing "Dixie," I do not have to fly the Confederate flag, I do not have to celebrate a war waged out of hate to be reminded that my mother makes the creamiest sausage gravy and the flakiest buttermilk biscuits. Or that the Crisco-laced skin of my grandmother's fried chicken will melt in your mouth. Or that there is no sweeter sound than the twang of a banjo married with a fiddle and the slap of a knee on a Satur-dee night. But to be Southern (to be American), I must acknowledge the black lives that had a profound impact on my history.

This remains a country in which Barack Obama is seen as a man who was white raised and white educated, a man who jumped through white hoops that are out of reach for many young black men—hoops that young women (both black and white) aren't empowered to even reach for. For the majority of their lives, black men and black women in America have been governed and educated by people who do not look like them. They have been raised in a country where secondary education confines their history to Frederick Douglass and Harriet

Tubman, to Rosa Parks and Dr. King, to the people who demanded freedom and equality, as though black history must be confined to slavery and segregation and to the overcoming of each—peacefully, mind you.

I assure you this essay is directed at no one other than at yours truly. The fact remains that I am a white man. And to understand how I view this world, I must acknowledge that every social and political platform, including Black Lives Matter, is a prism through which light can be shined. Yet we only see the color we want to, tilting every issue at just the right angle so that the light doesn't shine on the side we don't want to see. Having been raised and educated in the South—in Kingston, Tennessee, public schools during the 1990s and early 2000s—my only recollections of black culture in the form of literature are MLK's "I Have a Dream" speech and *To Kill a Mockingbird*, which was written by a white woman. I was a freshman in college before I purchased a book by a black author: James McBride's *The Color of Water*.

If I were appointed education secretary, I would require that James Baldwin's *Notes of a Native Son* be included in the curriculum of every high school senior in the United States. I am ashamed to admit, however, that even in the twenty-first century, requiring seniors in Small Town USA to spend six weeks on Baldwin would likely be met with the same resistance as spending six weeks on Darwin, or on the teachings of Gandhi, God forbid. Why does it have to be a black author, the thinking would go; why does it have to be about race?

Those same concerns have been raised about Black History Month every year since it was officially recognized by the US government in 1976. On Solange's album *A Seat at the Table*, her mother says she can't fathom how people can ask, "Why isn't there a white history month?" when all that's ever been taught in public schools is white history. She can't fathom how taking pride in black culture can be considered "reverse racism" when so many white people pay damn good money to hear Beyoncé and Solange sing. But even some black people worry about the implications of limiting black history to the shortest month of the year, worry that it segregates black history from American history.

Rarely does a black person arise in public secondary education unless he or she was an agent of drastic social change, or "the first" to accomplish a feat once thought incapable of a person with black skin. Meanwhile, white high school seniors are listening to Migos and Young Thug and Kodak Black in their headphones on the way to class, just as I listened to DMX and OutKast and Tupac in my Ford Focus when I was their age, cruising the streets of my hometown without a black person in sight. Outside the classroom, young white men and women mimic the dances and speech of black culture, sell out the shows of black entertainers, cheer on black pro athletes, and then go home to watch the news of another inner-city drug bust, the "carnage" in Chicago, and they begin to believe, as I did, that the extremes are the realities of black lives.

To be an American, I must acknowledge that the perpetuation of the black stereotype is a product of white America's refusal to teach black humanity in the classroom. I must acknowledge that inside me lies years of racial conditioning, thirty-plus years of being told directly and indirectly that black and white, like oil and water, can never truly mix. I must acknowledge that, as a white American male, black lives have been something for me to distance myself from, never someone to aspire to, and certainly not someone to love.

MAN IN THE (REARVIEW) MIRROR

...

On September 7, 2016, I decided to drive to the Grand Canyon. I woke up early, packed a suitcase, and booked a hotel room in Oklahoma City, a twelve-hour trip from Knoxville. My goal was to reach Flagstaff, Arizona, in two days. I did not know then that I wouldn't return home for two weeks. Or that my trek would include not only the northern and southern rims of the Grand Canyon but also the Pacific Coast Highway and Zion National Park in Utah.

During those seventy-five hundred miles, I streamed Travis Scott's *Birds in the Trap Sing McNight* and Frank Ocean's *Blonde* on a loop. I juxtaposed the messages of the two men—first, the "we made it" relief in the pre-Kardashian Scott's lyrics, the joy in his checks now being the size of what all women surely want between his legs, the joy in being able to have sex whenever he likes with a woman of any color, and having the money to buy whatever drug he cares to take, the dollars to buy whatever car or piece of jewelry his heart desires. Then there is Frank Ocean, who deftly weaves in and out of the rigors of fame, the confinement of gender roles, and the shackles of not only what white people see in his skin but also what black people see in his bisexuality. It is no mistake that the word *gay* is sung only once, on "Good Guy," a track that is just a piano-laced, a cappella interlude, a coming-out poem hidden inside a testosterone-laced hip-hop album.

Alone in my car for seventy-five hundred miles, I acknowledged that this is where and how blackness has existed for me—inside speakers, inside thumping bass lines and witty, tongue-in-cheek rhymes. Blackness has existed at a safe distance from me, where I can listen and visualize the struggles and the pain, the overt sexuality, even sympathize with not having a father during my teenage

132

years, yet never have to be personal with it. It has been purely voyeurism. During that thirteen-day road trip, I also acknowledged to myself that prior to driving for Uber and Lyft, only two black men had been in my car: a young man I played basketball with in high school and a friend of a friend in college. Prior to Uber, I had never had a black woman in my car; in fact, I have only been inside the homes of three black people in my life: all black women, all of them married to white men.

Color barriers are as comforting as they are confining, same as that literal wall President Trump would like to build. These figurative walls are all many of us have ever known, barriers that seem to have stood since the dawn, barriers that have been buttressed over and over by hate and by ignorance, but also by fear of the unknown that lies behind them. To bring down our barriers is to let the fear of the unknown inside. Whether that fear is real or imagined, we are not certain, but it is better to be safe than to be sorry.

When I returned from the West Coast, it was late September, and the skin of the South was beginning to tighten under the stress of a drought—hearts were just as tense, hands wringing over the fissures that were forming on the campaign trail. Hillary Clinton, we were told, was a shoo-in for the Oval Office. All logical signs seemed to predict a First Lady-turned-Commander-in-Chief, especially following the revelation on October 7, 2016.

The day before I boarded a plane to Italy, recordings surfaced of Donald Trump telling a TV talk-show personality that he could go up to women and simply "grab them by the pussy." The report prompted several women to speak out about alleged instances of Trump sexually harassing or assaulting them in the past. Surely, the proverbial nail was in the coffin. Surely, regardless of your pigment, the suggestion that a man running for Leader of the Free World would commit sexual assault removed all doubt.

While this essay isn't primarily about the degradation of women, I can't ignore that sexism and racism, while two separate evils, are not such strange bedfellows—as much as we'd like to keep each form of prejudice apart, not muddy the swamp. Yet how to separate the two in a man's mind, when the objectification of a woman is not confined to a color, when a white man's prejudice toward a black man is entangled with his insecurities over his own sexuality?

I can only view this world through the lens of a white, heterosexual male who was raised Christian in a small, nearly all white Southern town. With that one sentence, I am admitting the stereotypes I project onto others, assumptions that are then projected back onto me. My most influential exposure to black culture as a teenager was Tupac's *Greatest Hits* and the movie *Friday*, starring Ice Cube. My only tangible exposure to black culture was pickup basketball with the handful of black kids who lived on one street in my hometown, many of them defined by nothing more than nicknames: Gramps, a bruising running back who was the eldest; Byrd, a free safety who could fly; and Boomer, a shifty halfback you didn't get on the wrong side of. I was the white boy who would D up, hustle, crash the boards, and drive the lane with the same anger, "no blood, no foul." At school, we rarely spoke. They weren't invited to my house, and I never stepped foot in theirs. As for the few black girls I grew up with, the unfortunate joke was that they had no one to date because they were kin to all the black men in town—the unspoken fact being that no white man was allowed to cross that line, either.

Inside me live the very stereotypes I abhor. And perhaps there is no finer, more nuanced point to make: The root of the problem is in our own inability to acknowledge the systemic sexism and racism that has been buried inside us under layers and layers of religious and cultural ideologies. We are like drug addicts who must take the first step, admitting that we have a problem. But how to take the second step when everyone else is an addict too, many of us unwilling to admit we're thriving on an addiction to what we believe is the natural social order?

Not until I landed in Italy, only my second trip outside the United States, could I distance myself enough to have the self-awareness of my own skin. On my first day in Rome, I was stopped by African men who were wearing brightly colored kaftans and peddling bracelets. I eventually bought one: a piece of thick leather painted black, adorned with an oblong onyx stone in which a white elephant was carved. I gave the African man ten euros—half out of guilt for the lower class he portrayed, half out of guilt for my whiteness, the privilege my skin afforded.

But it was as if those African men capitalized on their skin in a way that wasn't shameful. They preyed upon the uncomfortableness of the American white man, who was not their oppressor but rather a tourist they'd been trained to exploit. Their color was secondary to the sale. There was no pride lost in assuming inferiority, if it meant euros to take home to their families. These black men seemed to have a different type of bitterness about their skin, for their plight was of no consequence to Italians. They had come to Italy on their own accord.

And thus the crux of the black-white quandary in the United States—the "what-if" of slavery. Black lives can't be extricated from

US history or culture. It's the same as a spouse who cheats on a marriage with children: There can be forgiveness, but there is no forgetting, and whatever the marriage might've been, it will never be again, nor will the children's lives ever be the same. A black person born in the United States must wake up to this forced union every morning, without the option for divorce. As Baldwin writes in "A Fly in Buttermilk," "I have not written about being a Negro at such length because I do not expect that to be my only subject, but only because it was the gate I had to unlock before I could hope to write about anything else."

As for me, I must write at such length about being a white man because I must face an unavoidable fact before I can write about anything else: The identity I inherited wasn't an identity at all, but rather a false notion of what constitutes being an "American." I inherited a racial identity predicated on a history of violence, of oppression and greed. I inherited a country both stolen from Native people and bolstered by the forced labor of enslaved people. This fact finally faced, I'm left with an unwelcome question:

What can a white man be if he can no longer simply be an American? ◆

One Year, 1,716 Rides, and a Crossroads

January 31, 2017, marked a year since I accepted my first Uber ride. It's cliché to say that it flew by. But it did. That first trip in Connecticut seems like another man behind the wheel, a man with no idea who he was or where he was headed. Which is probably why my first ride didn't go particularly well, although, in fairness, I was new to the concept of picking up a complete stranger and a bit anxious about my uncertain future. I had no source of income lined up other than my career as an Uber driver and the money I'd saved over seven years at ESPN.

If I'm honest, I didn't actually plan to drive for Uber for an entire year. At least not as my sole source of income. I didn't actually plan to start writing about the people I met, or about myself, or how my worldview began to evolve based on the lives in my car. Or that I'd build a website around the idea of my Existential Crisis, a year of travel and coming to terms with the errors of my past ways, a list that I'm still ticking off. But, as they say, one sin at a time. I could never have imagined that I'd accept 1,715 trips after that kid I picked up at the West Hartford mall, the one who accused me of starting the meter too soon, who cranked up the music in his headphones and didn't speak another word.

I also could have never imagined way back then that President Trump would be inaugurated. I planned to take a tack of open-mindedness with President Trump, with all the people, my family members included, who told me they had to live through eight years of Obama, so why can't I. I wanted this essay to be about all the slices of life I've ingested over the past year, all the sides I've heard and considered. I wanted this essay to be about how much hope my passengers have injected into me, not only for humanity but also for myself, a man who had begun down a path to complacency, a man who'd given up hope on much of anything.

I wanted this essay to be about one of my recent passengers, Tim, a thirty-something white man with a private pilot license, a guy with a chiseled jaw and a welcoming grin. He'd flown in from Louisville, Kentucky, after finding out his father had been rushed to the hospital in Knoxville with complications from cancer. I sped to the McDonald's drive-thru so Tim could pick up two Egg McMuffins—his dad's favorite, "Has to have 'em fresh," he said—and two large sweet teas. I agreed to wait at the hospital because Tim had flown in just to spend half an hour with his father. We bonded over the fact that I'd lost my father too, how you have no way of knowing exactly what you're losing until it's gone. I wanted this essay to be about a young black man who called himself "Dee," sporting a high-top fade and lugging his keyboard and beats machine, an aspiring producer/rapper. We bonded over one of our favorite hip-hop artists on the rise, Anderson .Paak, dissected his rhyme schemes and the beats he packages with colorful jazz riffs. We applauded each other, Dee and I, for following our passions, for choosing a road not necessarily less traveled, but a road that has no promise of a destination.

I wanted this essay to be about the stories that sustain us, the stories of people, just like you and like me. We the people of the United States. Anyone is allowed in my car. And if that person blows us up or kills me at gunpoint, then I will die knowing I did not discriminate against my fellow human being. That, to paraphrase ol' Dubya, is how we fight terror. Terror wins when we fear the unknown. Terror wins when we let the fear of fear itself prey on our better judgment, to paraphrase another of our former leaders.

But in light of President Trump's executive order to ban refugees and immigrants, and in light of Uber's weak response, I could not allow this essay to be tone-deaf, to land with a thud on levity. This essay could not be about the community Uber has created, not when Uber wasn't openly advocating to protect its diverse community.

When the New York Taxi Workers Alliance announced that it was implementing a one-hour strike at JFK airport in protest of the immigration ban, Uber alerted riders that "surge" pricing had been turned off and continued to allow drivers to collect fares. The hashtag #deleteUber began trending on social media, and many customers canceled their accounts in response. Meanwhile, Uber's competitor, Lyft, announced that it was donating a million dollars to the ACLU. I did not accept any Uber rides that day, mostly because I was attending my five-year-old nephew's birthday party in Nashville. I didn't drive the next day either, opting instead to catch up with a friend over, what else, beers and politics. While we talked, I received an e-mail from Uber's then-CEO, Travis Kalanick, outlining how Uber is supporting drivers affected by the ban, including the creation of a three-million-dollar legal defense fund to help with immigration and translation services. Still, Kalanick had already come under scrutiny for his relationship with President Trump and was scheduled to meet with the president that week as part of a business advisory council. In my estimation, hypocrisy is one of the world's most damning social ills, alongside dishonesty and disrespect, as a relative of mine likes to say. So was I a hypocrite to accept another dime from Uber?

People tell me I think too much. As if thinking—as opposed to not thinking—has put us in the predicament we are in. People tell me that I can't become obsessed with honesty and with truth. As if honesty and truth—as opposed to dishonesty and lies—have put us in the predicament we are in. People tell me that they appreciate what I'm trying to do, my sincerity, but that to be an open book 365 days a year is an impossibility. As if being sincere and forthright—as opposed to insincere and secretive—has put us in the predicament we are in.

My mother worries about her only child. My mother worries that I am going to write something on the internet or in a book that will follow me for the rest of this life, something that will disadvantage me in whatever career path I choose next. She worries I will turn a friend or a family member into an enemy. She also reminds me that I can let my unhealthy penchant for competition—to win—cloud my ultimate mission, which is to unite, not segregate. I wonder if that renders me just as polarizing and petulant as President Trump.

I wish my mother did not have a son like me, a son who has spent his life pushing people away out of fear that he might love them as much as the father he lost. I wish my mother did not have a son who has made an emotional island of himself, a man with no spouse or partner, a man with no child. I wish my mother did not have a son who believes that his purpose is to write what is in his heart. My mother raised me to have a big heart, a heart I'd closed. But that heart is open again, a heart so big that I'm not certain my chest can hold it some days, a heart that some days is so heavy I'd just as soon not have to bear it.

In my heart, I sincerely do not believe that President Trump is honoring the governmental processes of our great country. Or that he is showing any regard for the instantaneous and catastrophic impact his simple signature can have on human lives, both at home and abroad. So many people seemed to cast his first week in office in a positive light, as if he was finally greasing the slow-moving wheels of DC bureaucracy, as opposed to undermining the checks and balances of a democratic nation without its congressional consent. I've searched for the religious, honest man that his supporters have told me he is, searched to find him somewhere in his eyes, but to me they are as dark and unforgiving as a piranha's.

I am only an Uber driver, a thirty-one-year-old white man with a degree in journalism and an MFA in creative writing. I am not an expert on policy or economics or national security. I don't want terrorists in this country, same as I don't want to turn away refugees or immigrants at the door, with no care to where they're headed because we hadn't thought that far ahead. I'd like to have a president who would consider how to approach that statement reasonably, with thought and with care. But that's too reasonable a statement, it seems—a statement that doesn't seem to have any place in politics anymore.

It's no secret that I lean left, that I'll always err on the side of the individual over the populace, on the side of negotiation as opposed to aggression. President Trump has not given me any reason to believe he errs on the side of anything but his own whims, whether they align with his party or not. Our democracy, for now, remains intact, and I remain proud to live where I live, in a country where the gray area can still be seen, although the blues and reds are starting to bleed. You're free to vote for the candidate of your choice, or not to vote. You're free to march, or not to march. You're free to protest, or not to protest. You're free to volunteer, or not to volunteer. Just don't let that freedom become diluted, misconstrued as the right to ignorance, lest you become a detriment to our freedom as I once was, loitering for nearly all of my twenties as an uninformed citizen without a cause.

In the meantime, I'll give my Tennessee senators a ring, and I'll keep plugging away on my next essay and keep driving around my fellow Americans, listening intently to what they have to say. I'll keep volunteering for the Boys & Girls Club, and tonight I'm going to Yassin's Falafel House in downtown Knoxville to eat Mediterranean food and support a fund-raiser for refugees. I don't have as much as I once did, but I still have more than most. As for Uber, I refused to accept another ride, drove exclusively for Lyft, until after Kalanick succumbed to mounting pressure to leave President Trump's advisory council. I've had a lot of practice at being the problem. I figure it's time I start learning how to be the solution. ◆

Black Lives Matter

PART 3

My passenger had requested a pick up outside the Greyhound station on an eye-squinting, beaded-sweat kind of Wednesday in late May. When I pulled up, a tall, lanky white man was leaning against the red brick of the building. He wore a white tank top and faded blue jeans, and what wispy black hair he had left rested on the back of his head, unkempt. He shielded his eyes from the glow of mid-eighties heat, causing him to stretch his mouth and reveal an unhappy smile. Nothingness dotted the spaces where teeth had once been. Not six inches in front of him, a bald white man, also in a white tank top, reclined in a wheelchair, his thighs spilling over its sides, a crooked grin cemented on his face. His hands were folded over his bulbous belly, which gleamed from beneath the tank top and stretched the elastic band of his blue mesh shorts.

A thin black man, who looked much younger than the two white men, paced in front of the glass double doors to the station. His clothes were loose fitting, his dark jeans sagging around his hips, and he had on a plain black baseball cap, the skinny ends of braids curling out the sides and the back. My windows were up so I couldn't hear the exchange, but I watched the young black man untuck a cigarette from the side of his cap and show off a gold tooth while flicking his fingers. The lanky white man returned a gap-toothed smile and produced a lighter from the pocket of his jeans, reaching around the man in the wheelchair. The black man accepted the lighter and instantaneously lit the cigarette, inhaling a lung's worth of smoke. He returned the lighter and gave each man a fist bump, tugging at his pants and exhaling a white cloud as they all laughed. It appeared to be a genuine reprieve from the heat, and from the fact that all three were seemingly stuck on this sidewalk, just waiting for anything to happen, or for nothing at all.

I had received a Lyft request from Louis, a black man in his late fifties, or so I gathered from the headshot on the app, one of the differences between Uber and Lyft being the rider's ability to include a picture. It does help me, putting a face with a name instead of assuming what a person named "Louis" might look like. Yet, as vanity tends to go, people sometimes take liberties with their close-ups, same as the first date who doesn't provide a full-body shot on Tinder. But Louis emerged as advertised from the Greyhound station. He matched his photo almost eerily, as though the short-sleeve black polo he wore both in his headshot and in reality was his uniform. He strode across the sidewalk with purpose, not bothering to acknowledge the two white men and the young black man smoking a cigarette. They watched him, though, and I watched them watching him, all of us keenly aware that Louis was not one of them. Louis was not the aimless kind, nor did he have any time for exchanging pleasantries.

Louis's hair was cropped short and tight, and his chest and biceps were thick enough to stretch the shirt slightly. We connected eyes, his brown and sharp behind a pair of glasses. I attempted a welcoming smile, but he did not return it, only nodded and switched a black computer bag from his right hand to his left before opening the passenger's side door. His jeans were also black, and I considered then, as I studied the side of his goateed face, that his pigment seemed to fade into his polo and his jeans, as though he did not feel comfortable in any other color but that of his own skin.

"Where you in from?" I asked as I maneuvered out from the taxi line, leaving those other men in the rearview. I turned the A/C up a notch and left the music inaudible, waiting to determine if Louis was in the mood for conversation or a mindless ride. The rush of air sent a whiff into the car, a mix of men's deodorant and the sweat of a Greyhound bus, that faint stench of every other person who has perspired in that seat before you.

"Back from South Carolina," Louis said. His voice was measured, not gruff but not soft on the vowels, no use for any other words beyond the necessary ones.

"South Carolina home? Or Knoxville home?"

"Detroit's home," he said. Louis rested a hand on each knee, his board-like posture belied by his rounded shoulders and barrel chest.

"You taking a tour of the South?" I asked in an upbeat voice.

"No," Louis said. "I live here, lived here nineteen year." He subconsciously yet purposefully excluded the *s*, same as my grandfather does.

"I understand," I said. "Detroit's home home."

"Home home," Louis repeated. "But I'd just as soon not have another winter like a Detroit winter."

"I lived in Queens and Connecticut," I said. "Didn't know snow until then."

"This is home home, then," Louis said.

"It is," I said. "East Tennessee, anyway. I was raised in Kingston, went to college here in Knoxville. But home home feels a long way off, if you know what I mean."

"Wish I could say it gets easier," he said.

Louis didn't glance at me then as you might expect, with a nod or slight grin. I thought I caught him wince, a quick squint, but maybe it was just the sun, which had settled at eye level, an orange haze above the horizon. He looked straight ahead as the green exit signs passed on the interstate, signs that have become signifiers to me of who a person might be and how a person might live, depending on what neighborhood exit I take. I didn't know it yet, but Louis lived in a community of upper-middle-class condos about twenty minutes west of the Greyhound station. We were headed in the exact opposite direction of the barber shops and barbecue joints and gas stations with barred-up windows that line East Knoxville, where there is a high school on Martin Luther King Jr. Avenue. I'd admittedly assumed, when I first arrived at the Greyhound station and saw Louis's photo, that I'd be driving him to that side of town.

"What brought you South?" I asked.

"United States Postal Service," he said. "I requested a transfer and moved when I was fifty. I wanted to retire where it was warm. I have some people down here too."

"If my math's right, that makes you sixty-nine?"

"You right. I'll be sixty-nine in July," Louis said, and his mouth turned at the edges, although you couldn't call it a smile.

"You don't look sixty-nine," I said and meant it.

146

"They say black don't crack," Louis said, at least capable of some levity. "Spent forty-two years with the USPS; retired five now."

"Long time at one place," I said.

"Last of a generation," Louis said.

He turned toward me, let himself smile fully. Louis raised a hand off his knee and pushed the bridge of his glasses with his index finger, sliding them back on his ears. Then he brushed his goatee with a cupped hand before returning it to his knee.

"I couldn't even last eight years," I said. "Jumped ship at thirty."

"You don't look a day over twenty-five," Louis said.

"I'm thirty-two now," I said.

"What line of work?" Louis asked.

"Journalism," I said. "Sports journalism. ESPN."

I could sense him sizing me up, turning over a decision like that, to leave a solid career. If it wasn't for his black skin, Louis would've reminded me of my own father, his eyes scanning me from behind bifocals, searching for an answer to an obvious question.

"Awful good job to leave," Louis said.

"Feels like I need to apologize sometimes," I said.

"A man has his reasons," Louis said and raised a hand to readjust his glasses. He returned to his resting position, hands on knees, eyes as straight ahead as his back against the seat. "You got a plan?"

"If you would've met me a year ago," I said, "no clue." Louis's exit was approaching, so I checked the rearview and switched from the fast lane to the middle. "I was just back from Ireland, my first time outside the country."

"Looking for yourself," Louis said.

"For something," I said.

"It'll find you," Louis said, "if it's meant to."

"I'm moving to Atlanta soon," I said. "Going for my PhD in English."

"A doctor," Louis said, raising his eyebrows, leaning his head sideways. "Can't say I ever dreamed of such a thing."

"Can't say I did, either. I'm a writer, but no delusions of grandeur. I figure I might do some good in the classroom."

"I see," Louis said. "No wife, I assume. No kids. All these moves you makin'."

"You right," I said and smiled. I switched to the slow lane and merged onto the off-ramp. "I don't have an excuse or a reason. I lost my father at fifteen, and I've been looking for a home home I can't seem to find ever since."

"I had a boy," Louis said, unprompted. He rocked in his seat, breaking posture, his hands fidgeting across his knees. "But he died when he was six."

"I'm sorry," I said. "How . . ."

"Rare brain tumor," Louis said. "Nothing they could do. I still believe it was the Agent Orange." His voice returned to its measured staccato, the rhythm less steady, his tenor lower, tailing off.

"Vietnam," I said.

"Vietnam," Louis repeated. "Same reason for my diabetes. Just got diagnosed with early stages of Parkinson's, too. They decided it's all Agent Orange."

"You at least . . ."

"Compensated?" Louis interrupted again. "VA gives me a check every month. That must make somebody somewhere feel better."

I didn't prod any further, unsure of my place in the conversation, or where Louis had gone inside his own head. I was stopped at a red light, ready to turn toward the main highway, when Louis blurted out: "Our tank rolled over a mine. Blew it all to pieces. I had second- and third-degree burns, lost some of my brothers right there."

The light changed and I went left. "PTSD," Louis said. "Never will I go back there. All these great deals on tours and flights to Nam, telling me I should see how they've rebuilt the country, buried all those dead bodies. No, thank you. I'd just as soon spend a winter in Detroit."

The GPS recommended I stay straight, but Louis pointed for me to go right instead, and I did. "My grandfather was in Vietnam," I said, "the Air Force. He still sleeps with a noise machine, a pillow over his head, got so used to the bombs at night."

"The VA had me in therapy for a while," Louis said. "Big group of us, twenty or so, reliving all that mess. I was better off when I buried it. I quit goin'. They give me less money, but I'll take fewer nightmares."

"So you were drafted?"

"I enlisted," Louis said. "I didn't have no shot at an education. Didn't get one anyway, but thought it would be at the end of the line. I wanted to find out who I was, like you. I didn't know if I was black, or if I was a n---er or if I'd ever get another shot out of Detroit."

Louis dug his nails into his knees. "They knew what they was doin', convincing us broke kids we'd be put on a pedestal. Not much different than what they still doin' today, I guess."

There were so many questions to ask, and the journalist in me was riffling through them: Where did Louis stay while his wounds healed? Did he have any siblings? What of his mother and father? Why the post office? Where did he meet the mother of his child? What became of that woman? Had the death of their son hardened her heart and split them apart? Had the hate hardened Louis's heart, that same hate he surely felt for the whites who'd called him the N-word?

But the lives of my passengers can only be as long as the ride. I have to choose my questions both wisely and selfishly, because I rarely have the luxury of a follow-up session. These are the people I very likely would have never met if not for this modern-day hitchhiking, people who might never have opened up to me if not for these chance meetings, a trust predicated solely on human decency, that I will get them safely from one place to the next.

So I asked Louis, given that he'd actually lived through change, what he thought of our current predicament compared to the one he'd fought and nearly died for, possibly even lost his son for. I asked Louis, having said what he'd said about his own identity crisis, what advice he'd offer a young man without white skin in this America.

"What would I tell a black kid today? I keep my passport up to date," Louis said and smirked. He adjusted his glasses and rubbed his goatee. "I'm too tired to give much advice anymore," he said, pushing against his knees and leaning back, like he was relieving the pressure. "I've been answering for the color of my skin a long time. A long time. And if you're asking me, I'm not sure color has as much to do with our problems as we'd like to think. It matters, Lord knows it matters. But this is a class thing, if you ask me."

Louis looked directly at me for the second time, scrunching his forehead, gauging if what he'd said had resonated. "Ever been to Scandinavia?" he asked before I could return an answer. I shook my head no, keeping my eyes on the road. "I been a lot of places all over this world. Scandinavia is a place I could live. Closest I've seen to a classless society. About all of them white too. I hear that's changing, though."

"So no one ever stared at you there, cause you're black?"

"They stared," Louis said. "But they just hadn't seen no black people before. White people are always gonna stare. It's what's in their eyes that matters to me."

I clicked on my left-hand blinker, and the green arrow flashed a few seconds before I realized we were a traffic light away from the next turn. I tapped the gas and reached to turn off the lever, but Louis said, "Go ahead; more than one way to get there." So I cut onto a back road instead of the straight, ninety-degree angle up ahead, snaking through one of the many bluffs that have become suburban communities overlooking the strip-mall sprawl of West Knoxville.

The sun was sinking lower, setting the sky ablaze above the treetops. The white cotton of the clouds had gone a peach flavor, reds at the edges, dripping onto the soft greens of late spring. I took in a breath, wishing I could be content in this moment with Louis, to be certain that this path of mine—from East Tennessee to Queens to Connecticut and back—has been the correct one, so I can glance over my shoulder and find relief in how far I've come. I wanted to steer us away from the problems that have gained on us, or that never went anywhere at all. I wanted simple answers to put to rest the complicated questions, whether our problems are wrapped in race or in gender or in class or in religion, or if we're too wrapped up in all of them, if we're simply letting them confuse our judgment of basic rights and wrongs.

"What do you see in my eyes?" I asked. "I'm white." The shadows shifted around us with the swaying of the trees.

"You a good man," Louis said.

"Am I?" I said. "Cause it worries me. I worry a lot that my eyes are deceiving."

"That you can see that is the whole battle," Louis said. "Not half of it. We need more of that, Son. We need more thinking. But don't think you can fix it all alone. You can't save nobody from themselves."

"I hear you, about the class thing," I said. "You can always buy your way in, even if you aren't truly accepted. But aren't we still ignoring the answer to the question?"

"Which is what?" Louis asked.

"What does it mean to be *American*?" I said. "Do we *look* like Americans? Or is *American* a state of mind? Or is it just a piece of paper with a number on it?"

Louis was silent but nodded, like he was weighing his options. I assume Louis was like me, attempting to unravel those tangibles of class and race and religion and gender and sexuality that we've knotted up inside us, trying to untangle an identity that has become as elusive as terrorism, this need of ours to project fear and insecurity onto something un-*American*.

I asked Louis before he could answer: "What do you see when you hear *American*?"

Louis still didn't answer directly. He was a kind and considerate man, I could tell, see it when his dark eyes softened. He was a black man who'd started his journey on the lower end of life, and against the odds he'd risen to the middle, although not without casualty. Of course, I'm speculating, as I must do with all my passengers, but I'd say Louis had to hold his tongue far too many times along the way. I'd say that was why Louis had grown exhausted with discussing his blackness. He'd grown exhausted with his voice being drowned out by white noise, when blackness was never for him to come to terms with. He'd never made his blackness an issue. We had, and still do. However, Louis's blackness became an issue that could not be ignored as he continued his ascension to equal status, all of us—white and black—now chasing the "American Dream." I'd say that, if Louis were honest, he'd seen a white person flash behind his eyes when he heard me say *American*, because white is the only image this country has ever allowed itself to outwardly project—until Barack Obama challenged all we thought we knew about being an *American*. Louis knew that if he told me black was his *American*, then it would fly in the face of everything he and I had ever been taught, in school, in church, on the television. Louis pursed his lips, adjusted his glasses, and rubbed his goatee—a tic I'd picked up on, a tic that meant Louis was hesitant to engage but interested to hear where my logic was headed.

I'm the last person who should lead a discussion on US history, but I told Louis that I'd learned to put our Founding Fathers on a pedestal. I told Louis that I'd learned the ultimate position of power is president of the United States, and that the names I'd memorized as a kid in school were the names of white men, most of them Evangelical Christians.

"What if white people have confused being white with being American?" I asked.

"I do feel for white people," Louis said, "if they truly feel like they've lost their place. I know that feeling. That feeling of having nowhere to belong."

I told Louis I hoped he was aware of the absurdity, a black man commiserating with the very people who made him ashamed of his own skin. I fear those same white people still wouldn't give Louis the benefit of the doubt if they passed him at night on a street corner,

God forbid he have a hoodie pulled over his head. I fear that perhaps the real terror of white people lies in one day scanning a room and not seeing anyone like them—a concept as foreign as a black person on our currency, as foreign as peace riding on the wings of a crow and not a dove.

Louis motioned to the entrance of his condo community, and I recognized the name on the concrete sign welcoming us, a sign surrounded by manicured shrubbery and purple and red tulips. I'd been here before, and I'd always picked up and dropped off white people.

"What about you?" Louis asked. "You think you're losing your place?"

"Never felt like I had one to lose," I said. "I left the South and the church. Always figured I could come back anytime I liked. I even made my way to a tick above middle class. I'm back down now, though. But I haven't lost anything. If anything, I've gained perspective."

"Skin doesn't matter, then," Louis said.

"Maybe not," I said. "But you can dance, and I ain't got no rhythm. Right? You listen to Sam Cooke, and I love Skynyrd. You talk black, and I talk redneck."

"Stereotypes," Louis said. "Those are just problems if you let 'em be. People who get caught up in those aren't getting very far in this life."

"But when do the stereotypes become statistics?" I asked. "Are more black people in prison because they're more dangerous? Or have we just come to believe them to be more dangerous because we believe the stereotypes? How do I get to know Louis if I'm afraid of a black man getting in my car?"

"Think outside your box is what you're saying," Louis said. "Don't stay inside of a box cause someone says you can't leave it. And you did that, Son. Sometimes leaving your box is the only way to see the box you were in."

Easing through Louis's community, I noticed the condos were frame construction, straight edges and lines, the wood painted a muted beige. I was reminded of a short story called "Post and Beam" by Alice Munro, referencing a nearly synonymous style of construction. The story is about many things, but the conformity of the main character, a white housewife, is what stuck with me, how we often confuse the inevitably of our place in this world with the complacency to not question our place in this world, to simply live in the same style house—the same box—as everyone who looks like us.

I located the number of Louis's address, a freestanding condo with a single-car garage. I wondered if this was Louis's version of Scandinavia, a community where the exteriors were the same, a community where he could afford to be like everyone else, materially speaking. Louis had continued our discussion, circling around to class again, although I was only catching every third word, lost in my daze over how and why Louis had chosen his current residence, whether the black people in East Knoxville (back on MLK) would consider Louis one of them. Or if the people in this predominantly white condo development considered Louis one of them. I've lived in neighborhoods like Jackson Heights and Sunnyside in Queens, New York, where color lines blur easier, the majority morphing into the minority, depending on the subway stop. But here, in East Tennessee, it is virtually impossible for Louis to go about his day-to-day without encountering a white person; yet if Louis were to not leave the boundaries of West Knoxville, he could very likely not encounter another black person for an entire day.

I thought back to the one time I'd ever been the only white person in a room, at a TGI Fridays in West Philadelphia. I was staying at a nearby hotel and had wandered in after a concert. Only the bar area remained open after eleven, creating a club-like atmosphere. Most of the eyes swiveled to me, then quickly returned to their drinks and conversations. I nearly walked out, but I didn't want to feed any stereotype. So I found an empty high-top and ordered a beer and feigned interest in the NBA games on multiple flat-screens. No one spoke to me other than the server, nor did I strike up any conversations. I drank one beer as quickly as I could.

How many rooms had Louis been in as the only black man, where he wasn't wanted or wasn't allowed, bar counters and lunch counters where he sat because it was his right—but didn't make a sound because it might've meant his life? What does that type of exclusion do to a psyche? Why would Louis ever want to be in the same room with a white person again if it meant being inconspicuous, if it meant walking on eggshells to not feed into their stereotypes?

Louis pondered aloud about how Donald J. Trump had convinced so many people—people who will never shake hands with Trump's 1 percent—that a man born rich in New York City could unite a country divided along lines of wealth. "People of all colors bought into this, you understand?" Louis said, as if to prove his point about class trumping race. "Your education, that living you've been doing out there." He thumbed back to the exit like a hitchhiker. "That gives you *a* perspective. Emphasis on the letter *A*. You hear me, Son?" He went through his routine, glasses and goatee, although he added a stiff index finger pointed at me before putting his hands back to his knees. "Lot of people only have the perspective they're handed. You're figuring out where you fit, not letting the world peg you—middle-class, white, Southern, Christian, whatever."

I idled in front of Louis's muted-beige condo, letting the attaboy hang there in the silence between an older black man whose fatherhood was taken too soon and a younger white man whose father was taken too soon. In that intimate space, the space that shuts out the world's stereotypes, the colors did not matter, same as it seemed to disappear like that white cloud of smoke between two white men and a young black man back there in downtown Knoxville, in front of the Greyhound station.

What separated us from them was that Louis had the money for a Lyft, and I had the money for a car to give him one. Surely that was the answer, the class that divided us, put us in our separate boxes, not the color of our skin. But were we fooling ourselves? Would I have allowed Louis into my car if not for the pretense of Lyft? Or would Louis have even turned his dark eyes toward me if we passed on the street, an older black man and a younger white man with seemingly nothing in common, other than our beating hearts?

"You're the answer," Louis said, shaking a stiff index finger at me. He seemed to be uplifted by our crossing paths, or at least by what he and I seemed to stand for. Louis grasped his computer bag, adjusting his glasses. "Keep going out to meet the world; earn that beautiful thing called a perspective."

Louis extended his hand and I obliged, the kind of hearty handshake that I'd grown accustomed to in church, a hard squeeze more than a shake.

"What about you?" I asked. "What's your next chapter?"

I found out that Louis was also a driver for Uber and Lyft, and that he had a contract job driving commercial vehicles to pickup points across the United States, hence his return by bus.

"This retirement stuff's for the birds," Louis said. "Ain't got nobody keepin' tabs, so might as well see all I can see before I'm gone."

I was surprised that Louis had failed to mention our shared experience of Uber and Lyft, but to be fair, I hadn't asked. And I'd suspect that Louis is more of a listener, that I'd been given a rare glimpse into a man who prefers the solitude of the open road, considering he'd spent forty-two years confined to the post office, reading off addresses of places he'd never been.

"You a good man," Louis said again and loosened his grip. "I appreciate a man with a perspective." He let go and shut the door. He bent down and wagged that stiff index finger at me, then pushed his glasses up and rubbed his goatee and marched toward his muted-beige condo.

I wanted the conversation with Louis to end on that note, a tender and sweet one, so that we might be filled with the hope that sweet music brings. The melancholic truth in the words we'd spoken, the fact that we'd even had to speak them, to discuss the color of our skin, can certainly be hummed away if we'd prefer it that way, if we'd prefer our heads be suspended in the white clouds of sweet spiritual hymns.

As James Baldwin writes in "Many Thousands Gone," "It is only in his music, which Americans are able to admire because a protective sentimentality limits their understanding of it, that the Negro in America has been able to tell his story." Which I've always taken to mean that singing because you're happy and singing because you're free are mutually exclusive endeavors. I've always taken it to mean that singing was once as close to free, to living in the white clouds, as a black person could reach, a feeling that white people in America have never felt, nor can we fathom.

But I can't tickle any ivory, or strum a banjo, so I don't have a sweet melody to wrap around these words, to protect you from the silence in your own head, the discomfort you may or may not feel if you bother to determine what your color does or doesn't stand for in this country. I'm experiencing the same discomfort, writing these words alone and in silence, albeit from the safety of a laptop screen instead of saying them and staring into the whites of Louis's eyes. Louis and I were strangers, and while we had brought down barriers, there were entire lifetimes between us. We lacked that benefit of the doubt between two people of shared experience, the ease that exists between two people who know where the other is coming from, where the loyalty of the other man's heart lies.

I did not have the heart to tell Louis that my perspective remained unchanged, that once he emerged from my car, the world would still see him as a black man first, I believe, and would see me as a white man first, stereotypes included. I've spent years being convinced and conditioned—mostly by white people—to believe that color only matters if we allow it to, if black people allow it to, seeing as how they're the ones who are a different color, not us. I wanted Louis to be right, about the class thing, because he seemed so certain, like so many of his generation, that we'd moved beyond our pigment.

But when you are the change, as Louis was, it's often difficult to discern the miles left to go, considering how far you've traveled. I didn't have the heart to tell Louis that the majority of white people still do not know him, the middle-class black man, the one who served his country and put in forty-two years at the post office. That is not the black man who is portrayed on the TV. Louis is not the face of Black Lives Matter to white America. Those faces live on the South Side of Chicago, where stats conveniently support stereotypes. Or they are the faces of Steph and LeBron, or of Kaepernick and Kendrick Lamar, who do what white America believes black people have a predisposition to do. They are not the man at the post office, who'd like for his black life to matter as much as the middle-class white man who's certain Trump will restore America to when the instructions for his lawn mower were written only in English.

I didn't have the heart to tell Louis that you'd have to scroll to No. 100 on the *Forbes* world's billionaires list before seeing a black person, and that oil tycoon Aliko Dangote is Nigerian, not an African American. In fact, as of September 2018, you'd have to scroll to No. 480 before seeing Robert Smith, a Cornell grad and investor, the wealthiest black American on the list. Oprah clocks in at No. 887, while the only other African-American billionaire is Michael Jordan at No. 1,477. (For the record, President Trump ranks No. 766.)

Billionaire status is the kind of wealth that Louis and I will never know, and it is the kind of wealth that isn't for those of us in the middle to ponder, no matter our pigment, for it confuses our understanding of the lines. These people on the *Forbes* list, we are told, reside at the extremes, people who defy stereotypes and statistics, who pulled themselves up by their bootstraps, the people who prove class will ultimately define our perspectives and how the wider world perceives us. Yet surely even Horatio Alger could acknowledge the disparity on that *Forbes* list. Surely more black Americans than Oprah and Air Jordan and a man named Robert Smith would've pulled up their billionaire bootstraps by now.

And herein lies the truly blurred line—the fact that I'm sizing up people's identity based on the color of their skin in pictures on the internet, the fact that if Bill Gates's or Mark Zuckerberg's mother or father were black, our own government would allow them to check a non-white box, to say nothing of which "box" they'd choose, or which "box" would choose them. (Barack was half me, after all.) Right about now is when folks more educated than I, both black and white, would veer into a discussion about identity politics. And not that I don't have any use for real smart folks, but I would like to echo Ice Cube, who told Bill Maher on HBO that some white men (and women, I assume) have become too comfortable with using the word "n---er" because "you know, [they] might have a black girl-friend or two that made them Kool-Aid every now and then, and then they think they can cross the line."

So, you see, there is a line, despite Louis's belief that class has erased it. That is one of the great hoaxes Bill Maher and his upper-class, left-wing constituents have pulled off, committing a far graver sin than that of white, lower-class ignorance. They have become hypocrites, assuming that class and education (or having a black girlfriend who mixes up some Kool-Aid) somehow affords them the freedom to speak on blackness, as though they actually comprehend having black skin. Maher and his constituents have stooped to the same lows as their right-wing counterparts, those people who stereo-type black lives, who chalk them up to white statistics, even though those same white people don't want to be generalized as racist, or as people who ain't got no rhythm.

While hate is undoubtedly at the connotative root of the N-word, the concept of racism, even when explained to the blind man in part 1 of this trilogy, or to a child, must begin with the con-cept of skin color. After all, it is the body's largest organ. That is the inescapable reality—whether unspoken or laid bare, Louis and I are born into our skin and into a country that defines us by it, until we are given the opportunity to prove otherwise, an opportunity we might never be afforded. But for Louis, that has been a decades-long exploration and search, to quantify and qualify his blackness until he sees beyond his own skin to his own humanity. It has been a decades-long exploration and search that Louis was forced into, a journey he would never have set out on if he were white.

Before this year of my Existential Crisis, I had never even thought to ask the question "What does it mean to be white?" The question has been unnecessary, for it has long been answered inherently. To be born white (specifically white, male, straight, and Christian) in America has long been synonymous with being born *American,* with almost no concern for our ancestral roots. Any crisis of our identity does not worry with the color of our skin because we see our skin—within the confines of our own borders—as universal. Our crisis of identity begins and ends with our station in life, why we weren't born a Walton or a Trump, allowing us to repeat to ourselves that class is the ultimate arbiter. But the playing field will never be level until white people have to play from behind, until white people have to answer for the color of their skin. For there to ever be any shared experience, white people must experience the resentment that accompanies being judged by our whiteness, and the revelation that our whiteness both defines us and means nothing, and that it certainly does not make us Americans.

I began writing the coda to this trilogy from Kingston, Tennessee, nearly a week after giving Louis a Lyft. I was house-sitting and dog-sitting for friends while they went to the beach. One day I drove around my hometown in the sunshine, just to reminisce. I rolled down Greenwood Street, that quarter-mile or so where the few black people in Kingston lived when I was growing up, and where they still live. My father always told me that if I wanted to be a better ball player, then I ought to play on the court at Greenwood Street. Driving down it nearly seventeen years after his death, I'm not sure if my father was being racist, if he was just right, or both.

On Greenwood Street, there is a derelict-looking, two-story house that is a faded yellow. My mother would have yard sales when I was a kid to try to pay for a weeklong vacation to the beach, and three black women who lived on Greenwood Street would always show up. Once, my father and I hauled a dresser of ours to that two-story yellow house in his white Mazda pickup, and one of those women bought a Starter jacket of mine for her son, who went to school with me. I told my mother that I'd seen him wearing it, and she told me to never say a word about it being mine.

There is a church on Greenwood Street too, where my father sang with the black choir once. He'd been invited by the black woman who cleaned houses around town, including ours occasionally. She'd even babysat me a few times, although I can't remember her, only have proof of the woman in pictures. My father loved to sing old Southern hymns because he was born poor in Georgia in 1926 and picked cotton alongside the black people who sang those same hymns, the hymns that made my father happy and made those black people feel free. My father was respected by the people on Greenwood Street because he had paid some of their mortgages when he had the money, before he wasn't much better off financially than they were. When he died, some of them stood in the funeral line and shook my hand and told me he was a good man.

The basketball court is still there at the end of Greenwood

Street. It'd recently been repaved, although the lines had yet to be redrawn. Directly adjacent is a building that used to be the NAACP headquarters but appears abandoned now. There wasn't a soul out on Greenwood Street that day, other than two white men painting a handicapped spot in the small lot near the court, where I'd parked, a stranger to my past. The black kids I played ball with would emerge the minute my white friends and I had turned off our cars and started bouncing a ball. But I didn't have a ball, and I don't know where those young men are now. I've been told they work at local fast-food chains, or that they're in and out of jail. A couple of them are dead, but I hear at least one or two are doing all right, better than what could've been expected, white people say.

I walked the length of the court, wondering if my upbringing or my skin had been my ticket out. I wondered how those young black men must've felt, relegated to a single street in a small Southern town that remains 95 percent white. Had those black kids felt their place in this world predetermined? Had they played their hearts out on that court because it was the one place where they believed they were equal, where they belonged?

I wondered if Greenwood Street is an anomaly or remains a microcosm of our country. Am I the one living in the past? Will multiracial marriages render these sentiments of mine moot, as people have told me? Those same people have also told me that love trumps hate, that the generations over my shoulder won't be defined by color because color will become impossible to separate. Those black people who shook my hand in the funeral line and told me that my father was a good man didn't know that when one of my sister's kids, his granddaughter, dated a black man, he told my mother how much it bothered him, that he didn't like her mixing with black boys, not at all. I still cling to my own insecurities about potentially bringing home a woman of color to meet my mother and my grandmother one day, despite bringing them into my bed.

Standing on the court at the end of Greenwood Street, I closed my eyes and imagined us in perpetual motion, young black and white men, up and down the court, our focus on the orange ball and the red double-rim and the white net hanging against a blue sky. I opened my eyes and wiped away the water in them, tearing up over what we could not see then. We could not see in that rush of adrenaline how society had already pitted us against one another. We could not see how the wider world had already defined us—Southern and black and white and lower-class and middle, boys who would become men who should love women who are the same color.

I'd left this court, this town, this state, this country—I'd gained a perspective, yet we can never truly un-see how we first saw the world. Louis believes I am the answer, that I am a good man, like my father, yet I can never un-see the whiteness or the blackness or what the world has taught me to attach to it. Louis believes my acknowledgement is more than half the battle, yet I believe that the battle has only begun, that the battle is convincing people like me to acknowledge their racist perspectives. And there is no battle more daunting than convincing people to acknowledge their own hatred, and then to let go of it.

As Baldwin writes in "Notes of a Native Son," people cling to their hates so stubbornly because they sense that once hate is gone, they'll have to deal with pain—the pain of admitting, against all logic and human decency, that we've allowed the color of our skin to dictate whether or not a person is worthy of being human, is worthy of our respect, and our love. ◆

An Ode
to Alcohol

When people get in my car, they often ask, "What's your craziest story?" Friends ask me the same question. They all assume that one of the few reasons to request an Uber or a Lyft is because you're headed to get drunk, or you're too drunk to drive home.

There is truth to that. Although I've given more than two thousand rides and most of them have been of the sober (or, at most, buzzed) variety. I have a nearly religious cutoff time of midnight, too. I enjoy this job, and while there is more money to be made after last call, I avoid the graveyard shift out of fear that I might no longer enjoy this job. People recalibrate their inhibitions when they're drunk. People vomit when they're drunk. I've been those people.

Sure, the "fun drunk" does exist, and I have plenty of those stories that I haven't bothered to write down. Like Rick, for instance, the white guy in the tattered, faded Atlanta Falcons jersey. I picked him up after Super Bowl LI, the night the New England Patriots made a historic comeback to stun Rick's team. I arrived in downtown Knoxville to find him standing outside an empty bar smoking a cigarette. He didn't notice me at first, blowing smoke and staring into the void of an epic loss. I rolled down the window. "Rick?" He shook his head yes and stamped out his cigarette with his foot.

Rick was painfully defeated, and I realized he was also inebriated once he slurred his first, "Fuckin' Tom Brady." Rick let out a shoulder-shrugging sigh. "He's the goddamn greatest." Rick took off his glasses and ran his fingers through the receding red stubble on his head. Then he quickly put his glasses back on. "Fuck. That. Guy." He poked holes into the air with his right index finger to help punctuate each word.

Rick was entertaining in that die-hard fan way, a man-child wallowing in the inexplicable loss of his boyhood team. It was a "how could we let that happen!" diatribe at its finest, complete with the hypothetical logic: "If we would have done this!" or "If we would have done that!" when, in the end, the game is over. Rick wasn't belligerent, just disappointed, and over the course of the twenty-minute ride, I gathered that this was a rare night of excess. He was the head chef at a locally owned restaurant on the west side of town, and he told me he'd spent his entire adult life in the food business, starting at seventeen as the grill cook at a Sonic Drive-In.

"One Super Bowl I was working at Hooters for Christ's sake," Rick said, turning his palms and his eyes toward Heaven, or whatever he believed was up there. "I was their best damn cook, so they put me on fuckin' wing duty. I went to sleep still doing this shit." He began moving his arms in small circles, like he had a metal bowl in each hand, tossing wings in hot sauce. "If you can work the wing station at Hooters on Super Bowl Sunday, you can do anything. Fucking anything." Rick quit moving his arms and swatted the air as if to say, "Brother, please."

For reasons I couldn't follow, Rick's friends had switched locations before he'd shown up downtown. So Rick, being a true Falcons fan, opted not to bar hop and relished the relative quiet of a place known more for cocktails and bruschetta than lite beer and wings. He could watch a flat screen without distraction, order a beer on demand. But when the Falcons let their lead disappear, Rick only had the alcohol and the bartender to commiserate with in his disbelief. It was sort of depressing, this forty-something man going home drunk to an empty apartment, in desperate need of a warm body and having to settle for a twenty-minute ride with me.

But even through the drunken haze that hangs over a person, you can catch a glimpse of a man's heart. Rick was all right, probably the same earnest, endearing man sober as he was drunk—just less demonstrative and introspective, maybe not as quick to drop the F-bomb. He was a man who hadn't let the hops and mash mix into anger, the way so many men do when they live and die by the results of a game.

I have shared encounters less tame than the one with Rick, in private, while having a beer with friends. They laugh out loud, my friends, and they ask me why I don't share *those* stories on the internet, instead of writing ad nauseam about Donald Trump and Black Lives Matter.

But it's all in the delivery, isn't it? I can make a story smack of sentimentality. Very rarely do I show the unfiltered worst of a person, especially a person not in complete control of his or her faculties. While it isn't my job to protect people from themselves, I'm disturbed by our growing fascination with a person's low point, our inability to turn our heads from a train wreck, perhaps taking some morbid sense of solace in the fact that at least it wasn't us.

I picked up two drunk women recently at a country-western club in way west Knoxville, the Cotton Eyed Joe, so named for the popular song and line dance. I'm conflicted because of how drunk the women were and how embarrassed they'd be if they read about that side of themselves. Of course, the same could be said about anyone I've written about. But it's not you and it's not me, is it?

The Cotton Eyed Joe exists in the recesses of my mind as one of the last bars where life floated along in that smooth simplicity of youth. It's a club that thrives on its own self-aware cliché, the J and O on the neon red-and-blue sign shaped like a cowboy boot and spur. The unofficial dress code for women consists of cowboy boots and short, flowing dresses or Daisy Dukes. The men occasionally oblige with boots and snug Wranglers and a tucked-in Oxford and a cowboy hat, maybe a bolo tie if they've pre-gamed enough.

My buddies and I never acted the part. We'd only drive the twenty-five minutes from the University of Tennessee campus to West Knoxville on a Sunday night for the "free dance," when the DJ wasn't confined to the do-si-do. Well, that and the free beer. There was a cover charge, but every Sunday after midnight pitchers of the most watered-down lite beer were zero dollars. We'd show up at 11:45 and drink till last call, which was around 3:00. I was the only one who'd act a fool, falling in with the solo line dances, old favorites like the Electric Slide and, of course, the Cotton-Eyed Joe. I'd like to tell you that I chased every clear plastic cup of Natty Light with a cup of water, or that I sweated out enough of the alcohol to sober up for the drive back to campus during those pre-Uber, pre-Lyft days. But I won't.

I haven't been back inside the honky-tonk since I left Knoxville in the summer of '07, and in the year since my return, I've only had one ride request to the Joe—a group of foreign exchange students, all of them women from Germany, who wanted to see "real" cowboys. But on a recent Saturday night, the same night Drake's new album, *More Life*, was released, I received a Lyft request to an address I didn't recognize until I spotted the neon red boot and spur en route, rising just above the tree line along Interstate 40. It was nearing my cutoff hour of midnight. I sat in the parking lot and spun the proverbial roulette wheel of scenarios in my head, wondering why "Denise" would hail a ride nearly three hours prior to closing time.

Three middle-aged men wearing ten-gallon hats were perched on stools at either side of the two entrances, one for eighteen-and-under, the other for twenty-one-plus. They were swapping bouncer stories, or maybe marveling at the warm March weather, soaking in the calm before the Saturday night stampede of drunks stumbled out in droves. Finally, two white women emerged, visible for a brief moment in my rearview. At night, I rarely get a close-up of my passengers. My attention is elsewhere, confirming the destination on my app, cueing up the GPS on my phone, before navigating my way out of strange driveways or apartment complexes or parking lots. I don't have a chance to look them over, basing my initial assumptions on name, location, and tenor of voice.

Denise and her friend weren't wearing Daisy Dukes, I did notice that, but both were wearing short dresses. They sat in the backseat and were strangely silent for having just exited a club at nearly 1:00 in the morning. Before I was out of the parking lot, Denise said,

An Ode to Alcohol

"Excuse me, where are you taking us?" She smacked her lips open and shut, a distinct pause between clauses, like she was irritated at me over a destination I didn't choose.

I fought the urge of a smart-ass reply, calmly reading off an address that was just a few minutes away. As if she didn't remember entering the address, Denise let out an "ugh" and slapped her friend's knee.

"Can you give him the address?" Denise demanded more than asked. "We need to go back to her house. I can't be without my fucking car. I told you we'd get stuck there."

The friend was giggly and chipper, reciting the new address, which was in a town over, roughly twenty more minutes farther west of where we already were.

"We should just go downtown," the friend said. "Forget about it—we can get the car in the morning."

"No," Denise said. "Fuck that. We're drunk."

"You're drunk," the friend said and giggled. "I would've stayed."

"Bitch, you weren't gonna get laid," Denise said, teasing in her voice, although I could detect an edge of resentment too, like maybe the night's plan hadn't gone how she'd predicted.

"Don't blame me for being a lightweight," the friend shot back. "Them boys were all up on me, and I wasn't ready to leave."

"What the fuck . . ." Denise said and paused, ". . . are you talking about?" The *about* tumbled from her lips, like the *b* had tripped over her tongue. She'd gone from a relatively harmless zero to a volatile sixty in the time it took me to drive to the main road, only about a quarter-mile. "You weren't goin' nowhere but an empty bed."

"Let's go downtown and see," the friend said, either oblivious to the condescension or too drunk to care.

I was nearing the interstate on-ramp when Denise blurted out, "Take us to Taco Bell."

"Rude, party of one," the friend said and snorted as she laughed.

"Um, please," Denise said.

"Like you need something to eat," the friend said.

"You're no skinny bitch," Denise said.

I did as I was told, never one to not oblige the passenger, especially not a drunken one, similar to tiptoeing around a child's potential tantrum, not wanting to shift Denise's drunken attention to me. I couldn't yet piece together the dynamic between the two women, or why it was they'd gone to the Cotton Eyed Joe, or why they'd left early. They were friends, or at least this routine didn't seem new.

The Taco Bell drive-thru was six or seven cars deep, and Denise's friend asked if she could smoke a cigarette. It's a bold ask to make in a nonsmoker's car, and I've only been faced with it on a handful of rides. I reluctantly said yes, as I have on the other occasions, not particularly keen on confrontation, even when it relates to something as innocuous as telling a person I'd rather the stale smell of smoke not settle into my leather interior. But I've always preferred people I've never met to consider me "cool" or a "nice guy," reinforcing my own self-image, often to the detriment of people who have to see me more than once.

"Just keep it out the window as much as you can," I said.

"You know he really doesn't want you to," Denise said.

"He just said I could."

"You don't pick up on shit, do you?"

"You need to get laid," the friend said and laughed and snorted.

I cracked a smile myself. Then I heard more of a slight pop than a smack and looked up in the rearview as Denise was retracting her hand from her friend's face. The friend let out a few staccato giggles of shock. I'd obviously never met the two women, so every hole of their story I fill in is merely a hunch, or perhaps a projection of my own experiences. I assumed then that Denise and the woman smoking a cigarette, both in their mid- to late twenties, were relatively recent friends, probably friends in the way that they'd traveled in a similar weekend social circle, deciding to split off as a duo on non-partying weeknights.

Denise hadn't hit her friend, not in the traditional sense, just pushed her friend in the cheek, enough to turn the woman's head. This was a side of Denise the friend hadn't seen, and in that instant, I could sense that the friend had already begun to retreat emotionally, aware of the friendship's limitations.

"What do you want?" Denise asked.

We were next up to order, but the friend didn't immediately answer, still reorienting herself. Denise had put the confrontation behind her as if it had been a natural reaction in the course of conversation. Her actions, in her own mind, weren't attached to any consequence or reality, only her childish need for retribution, her focus now returned to the hunger pangs.

"I don't need no damn taco," the friend said.

"Just order something, dammit," Denise said, craving a companion to justify the calories. I'd pulled forward so that Denise was face to face with the intercom.

"Ma'am, please don't cuss in my ear," the disembodied voice said sternly.

The friend laughed, still buzzed enough to find the sophomoric exchange entertaining.

"I apologize," Denise said. "My friend's had too much to drink."

"Can you believe her?" the friend said, projecting the question at me.

"What do you want, what do you want, what do you want!" Denise pouted. "We're not moving until you order."

The situation wasn't yet dire enough for me to intervene, or to remind Denise that she wasn't in control of the brake pedal. "Fine," the friend said. "One of those bell nacho things."

"OK," Denise said into the intercom. "We want a bell nacho and . . ."

"Ma'am, we ain't got no bell nacho," the woman said.

"Nacho Belle Grande," I said.

"Yeah, that," the friend said, giggling.

"Thank you, sir," Denise said, as if she were addressing me for the first time. "We want a Nacho Belle Grande . . . and I want a . . . bean burrito."

"Oh my gosh," the friend snorted. "More like a diarrhea burrito." Denise stayed facing the intercom but reached behind and swatted her friend's leg. Her friend high-pitched laughed at this, saying "Ow," as if they were two kids tickling one another, faux fighting.

"And can I get an order of cinnamon twists and a caramel apple empanada? And a Diet Mountain Dew to drink?"

"Like a regular Dew matters after all that," the friend jabbed.

"That's it," Denise said.

The woman repeated the order and gave Denise the total. The banter had nearly cleared the line ahead of me, creating a disproportionately long line behind me.

"What if I wanted a drink?" the friend said.

"Shut up," Denise said.

"I should've gone downtown by myself," the friend said.

"She's too drunk to go anywhere, isn't she?" Denise asked rhetorically.

"I'm the wrong guy to ask," I said.

"You're a nice guy, aren't you?" the friend said. "I can tell nice guys."

"Would you quit hitting on everything with a dick," Denise said.

The friend giggled again to circumvent further insult. I wondered if her response was one of admission, or a learned response to hostility, a defense mechanism to avoid verbal exchanges that could reveal her insecurities.

I pulled to the second of two windows, and Denise handed the woman her card.

"Sauce?" the woman asked.

"Sauce?" Denise asked her friend.

"I didn't even want the nachos," the friend said.

"Hot and fire," Denise said.

"I'm not passing out next to you tonight," the friend said. "Look out below!"

"I'm so sorry for her," Denise said as the woman handed her the bag and drink. "You have a good night now."

I rolled forward but Denise told me to stop.

"I don't trust them ever," Denise said, rummaging through the bag to double-check her order. "OK. You can go."

I heard Denise tear open what I assumed was the bean burrito. She went quiet. I'd kept the music nearly inaudible, and Drake's album was nearly halfway through. I clicked to track three, "Passionfruit," and turned up the volume. The friend wasn't smoking anymore, but her window was down. The air was balmy. I opened my sunroof as I merged onto the interstate.

"Oooh," the friend said as the Latin backbeat found its stride, a half-step too slow for the salsa. "Turn. This. Shit. Up!"

I did, loud enough that Drake could be heard above the wind whipping through the car. I was relieved. Denise was occupied with her burrito, the friend was shimmying in her seat, and I could cruise uninterrupted for fifteen minutes, no more listening to two drunk women bicker. My reprieve barely lasted a full song:

"So, what do you do?" the friend yelled, leaning up between the seats. I have a stock explanation for the Existential Crisis—leaving ESPN, traveling for a year, coming to terms with mistakes. But I wasn't in the mood for the dramatic Q&A that would surely ensue.

"I had a decent job for a while in the Northeast," I said, not yet conceding to turn down Drake. "I saved my money. Decided I wanted to travel for a year, so I left."

"Then why the hell did you come to Knoxville, Tennessee?" the friend yelled.

"Close to home," I said.

"Why'd you ever leave if you love it so much?"

"Wanted to get away from it," I said. "See if I really loved it."

"Where all'd you go?" she asked. I lowered the volume, realizing there was no wearing her down.

"Ireland, Italy, out West," I said. "Just spent a lot of time with me, myself, and I. We had a lot to talk about."

The friend giggled and put her hand on my shoulder. "I'm saving right now too," she said. "To see the world."

I was nearing the fork where Interstate 40 and Interstate 75 split, the former headed west toward Nashville, the latter headed south toward Chattanooga. The GPS told me to veer toward Chattanooga, but I grew up in a town on the way to Nashville, and you can get there either way. So I asked, "Toward Nashville, right?" and the friend said yes.

"What the fuck?" Denise screamed through a mouthful of bean burrito. "Chattanooga, you idiot."

"Sorry," I said. "I was raised in Kingston. Just used to going that way. You from here?"

"Hell no," Denise said.

"I'm from Georgia," the friend said.

"California," Denise said.

"Then why in the hell did you come to Knoxville, Tennessee?" I said, mocking the friend.

"A change," Denise said. "Sometimes you need a change."

"What about you?" I asked the friend.

"Same," was all she said.

"So what're you running from?" Denise asked.

"Myself," I said.

"I'm running from everyone else," the friend said and laughed.

"You two are ridiculous," Denise said.

"Why are you so special?" I asked.

"I came here for a guy," she said. "It didn't work. You move on. No big fucking deal."

"I was actually out your way back in September," I said. "I drove from here to San Francisco, all the way up the PCH."

"How cool," the friend said.

"I've done it," Denise said, "a few times."

"How'd you two meet?" I asked.

"Me and the guy?"

"No," I said. "You two in the backseat?"

"Oh, we're bartenders," Denise said. "Well, I'm a bartender; she waits tables."

"You like driving for Uber?" the friend asked.

I said that I'd been driving for more than a year without complaint. But I told her she was technically in a Lyft.

"Yeah—I'm fucking paying like forty-five dollars for this," Denise said, chomping down the remains of the bean burrito, then crumpling the wrapper. "Fucking Uber wouldn't take my card or whatever the hell. You owe me, big time."

Denise wasn't paying forty-five dollars, but she was in no state, nor was I, to explain to her that Uber and Lyft are virtually the same app and virtually the same price. I steer the conversations, same as I do the car, and I've been around enough drunks to know that the war is getting them home without incident. So any battle not directly related isn't worth fighting. Denise could've said the capital of California is San Francisco, and I wouldn't have disagreed.

The silence settled in again as we neared the exit. I pushed the volume up on my steering wheel, letting Drake drown out whatever discussion Denise and her friend were having, something about staying overnight, not being able to drive, the friend insisting she was OK to. They reluctantly agreed on the smart choice. After a pause, the friend tried to whisper, "Check your phone." But the alcohol had rendered her unaware of her decibel level, like someone wearing headphones and screaming over music no one else can hear. "I sent you a text."

"Whatever," Denise said. "Whatever the fuck you want."

"What do you think?" the friend asked in the same failed whisper.

"You're an idiot," Denise said.

The text wasn't any of my business, nor did I want it to be. The four-lane highway running through the town they'd found themselves in was empty, fast-food signs and car lots gone dark. The town has grown in population over the past decade, which in Small Town USA tends to mean a new factory or two, which begat a few more restaurants, which begat a bigger high school gym or football stadium. But its small-town roots remain intact, Knoxville still the "big city," the Cotton Eyed Joe as far as some are willing to venture. The bars and clubs of downtown Knoxville might as well be as far away as California.

I turned across the opposite two lanes of highway onto a side street that curved around to an apartment complex. Denise was digging through her purse, the Taco Bell wrappers rustling.

"Where are the fucking keys?" Denise said in drunken exasperation. "Did you get them from her? Fuck. Text her. If we don't have those fucking keys."

"I thought you put them in your purse," the friend said. "I never had them. You're the one who wanted to leave."

"Way to help," Denise said. "Way to help. Thanks for that." I parked the car in an empty space and was idling. A light appeared in my rearview. Denise was using the flashlight on her phone, but it was aimed at the darkness in her purse casting shadows across her face, which was oblong and mostly covered by strands of smooth black hair, her complexion olive, her features harsh and scrunched in irritation.

"Thank. Christ," Denise huffed. "Found them. I'm out."

Denise grabbed the Taco Bell bag, and what was left of the Diet Dew sloshed in the cup. She opened the door and slammed it shut. I watched over my shoulder as she walked to the complex, not looking back. Denise was tall and rail thin, despite her friend's claim that she could do without the bean burrito.

"Hey," the friend said. "Do you go out?"

The car was dark except for the greens and blues glowing on my dash. She'd leaned up in the seat, her stale breath grazing my ear, a hint of fruity liquor in my nostrils.

"Now and then," I said.

"Like you drink and dance and stuff?"

"I've been known to."

"You want my number?" she asked.

"Um, sure," I said. "Never can have too many friends."

"Put it in your phone," she said.

I removed my phone from the holster on the dash and opened my contacts as I felt her lean forward, peering over my shoulder.

"Wait, you haven't even seen what I look like," she said. She opened her door, clicking on the interior lights. "Look," she said. I craned my neck and left my eyes on her for a few seconds, hoping I wasn't tipping my hand one way or the other. I could describe this woman for you. I could, but I won't. You're already embarrassed for her, just as I was then, the alcohol clouding her judgment of the situation.

I will admit that Denise was more attractive to me physically, and that if this woman had looked like Denise, I would've been less hesitant to put her number in my phone. There is a shallowness to that admission, yet that is the sobering reality. You could argue that I should've declined her number, not given her false hope, although what would you do in the situation? Would this woman even remember me in the morning? What if the roles were reversed, a man hitting on a driver who is a woman?

I turned to my phone. "What's your name?"

"M . . . E . . . G," she said. "They call me Meg."

"Meg," I said. She recited her number as I typed. "Got it."

"Text me next week," Meg said. "I'm a good time."

I nodded and smiled. Meg lingered for a reply, then climbed out. She called after Denise, "Score."

I told the heavily abridged version of that story to two friends at a bar, two women. They laughed at the dynamic, the "asshole drunk" friend versus the "silly drunk" friend. They laughed at "diarrhea burrito" and at the number of F-bombs dropped by Denise. They laughed at the whispers that weren't whispers and Meg's bold move.

In fairness, the hilarity of Denise and Meg is, of course, in the recognition of the caricatures—the "I've been there before" connection the two women hearing the story have with the women in the story. That is not lost on me. I can also relate, or commiserate, as the case may be. I can't help but wonder, though, if our fascination with the inebriated doesn't ignore what has driven two women, or anyone, to drunkenness. We soak up what transpires without bothering to consider the disregard for self-control and the demons that led to the dangerous excess.

There is an inherent sadness to Denise and to Meg, the woman suppressing a rage that bubbles over when fueled by alcohol and the woman perhaps selling herself short, searching for a guy to text her, a friend to treat her with respect, relying on liquid confidence to convince herself she deserves both. I don't find much humor in that. I've given too many rides to too many women and too many men and heard them say words that I can't repeat. I've seen a woman go limp in my backseat, dead weight to the point that I had to help her male friend drag her up apartment steps. If I find anything in those people anymore, it's humanity, it's in the self-inflicted pain, in the tangible struggle of one day to the next, however it is you can manage to get there.

I know that struggle. I've been drunk in a lot of bars—across the Southeast, the Northeast, and out West; bars in Chicago and Milwaukee, pubs in Ireland and bars in Italy. I broke my finger while riding a mechanical bull in New Orleans. (For the record, I went longer than eight seconds.) But it all started here in Knoxville, Tennessee, during my four years as an undergrad, when I still had to chug a beer and slosh down a shot, unable to appreciate the bittersweetness of each sip. It's where I first experienced what anyone who's spent any time in bars refers to as "whiskey drunk," that stage when the senses slur as much as the words, when the emotions spill out, right along with the vomit. Some of those nights in those bars aren't so much memories as stories that are recited as folklore about a young man I used to know.

There's a dive bar on Manhattan's Lower East Side where I once ordered the "PBR and a shot" deal three times too many. I was later told that I said to a man who was harmlessly hitting on my ex-girlfriend that I would end him. I grabbed him by the shirt collar and poked him in the chest and actually said, "I will end you." Apparently, the man must've seen something in my eyes to believe that I would, although I'd like to believe that was the Jack talking. I can't rightfully say for sure, even now, because I'm not sure I could tell you what the young man inside those eyes was even thinking, or if I would even recognize him anymore.

I'm not a rarity in that regard. I've driven around enough sloshed twenty-somethings (and thirty-somethings and forty-somethings) to no longer care or worry about people looking down from whatever false pedestal they stand on. Perhaps that unidentified anger and vindictiveness lies dormant inside all of us, in that confounding blur of youth that we often never grow completely out of. The liquor simply awakens it, manifests it in forms out of character, or in character that we have yet to face, a side of ourselves that we spend a lifetime avoiding.

Matter of fact, I'm drinking a beer right now, as I write the epode to this impromptu ode. I can't sleep. I'm taking the edge off, as some might say, quieting the voices that can become deafening and debilitating, the voices that speak these words I write to you. When I was twenty-three, I was arrested for public intoxication, and then I wrote a cover story for an alternative newspaper about my nearly forty-eight hours lost inside the Knox County jail system. When I was nineteen, I pleaded guilty to criminal impersonation for entering a bar with a fake ID. If you're keeping score at home, the charge was removed from my record after eleven months and twenty-nine days of being "crime free." I've never been charged with driving under the influence, although that just means I haven't been caught. I don't owe you any of that, but to write about Rick and Denise and Meg, to write about drunk people with any level of sincerity, or dare I say humor, I must acknowledge my existence on the other side of the story. Or risk perpetuating the hypocrisy that comes with diagnosing social ills while still partaking in them. It's easy to point and giggle when your head isn't hovering over the toilet.

Nowadays I rarely get as drunk as that young man I used to be on the Lower East Side. On the occasion that I do, I tend to be as nostalgic and sentimental as Rick, reciting the places I've lived and traveled, the friends I've made and miss, the voices I'm not likely to hear again. I tell people that I wish I would've been inside myself for more of those moments, sober for a life that I can't ever relive. That will always be my regret, that many of the moments I hold dearest are drunken vignettes singed at the edges, like old photographs salvaged from a house fire. ◆

Goodbye to (Most) All That

It is easy to see the beginnings of things, and harder to see the ends. I can remember now, with a clarity that makes the nerves in the back of my neck constrict, when New York began for me, but I cannot lay my finger upon the moment it ended, can never cut through the ambiguities and second starts and broken resolves to the exact place on the page where the heroine is no longer as optimistic as she once was.

—JOAN DIDION, "Goodbye to All That," 1967

I'm sitting at LaGuardia Airport, drinking a laughably overpriced pale ale and waiting to board my return flight to Tennessee. These past five days were my first in New York City strictly as a tourist. I booked this trip a couple of months back, after learning that I had secured a position as a graduate teaching assistant and PhD student in creative writing at Georgia State University in Atlanta. These five days, for me, were to be both a celebration and the culmination of what had amounted to eight years of my life, from twenty-two to thirty, unknowingly spent pouring my own mold that I plan to fill on my own terms in the decades that are hopefully ahead.

I lived in this city for roughly three of those eight years, and one of my ex-girlfriends had a studio here for three more, splitting our relationship between Brooklyn and the condo I owned in Hartford, Connecticut. Six years is a relatively short existence, but it is also 2,190 days that made up most of my twenties, that decade when you're unleashed into the wide world without an instruction manual, or a guide for what to expect should your priorities and moral compass unexpectedly shift.

I didn't have a set itinerary, other than taking a day to drive a few hours north to visit ESPN in Bristol, Connecticut, to give hugs and handshakes to my friends and mentors there. I was also determined to go as high up in the Empire State Building as I could. Despite having worked on 34th Street between Fifth and Madison, I hadn't been inside the lobby, much less to the 102nd floor, about a quarter-mile above that vast expanse of steel and concrete known as Manhattan, which was originally *Manahatta*, or "hilly island" in the language of the Lenape people, who inhabited the land before the first white man or skyscraper.

Mostly, though, I'd planned to eat good food and drink good drinks at restaurants and bars that I once couldn't afford, and then I could, and soon wouldn't be able to again. I ate and drank with friends who've known me since I showed up with only two suitcases, friends who now give me a corner to drop my bags and a couch to lay my head, the kind of friends who heighten the senses and cause the food to taste better and the drinks to seemingly never run out. And I texted two women, two women who didn't owe me absolution, but whom I at least owed some amount of closure. I shared laughs with each of them, and in the silences I believe there was forgiveness, an understanding that even though fond memories can be tainted with bitterness, it's a taste worth acquiring, so as to not wipe out the sweetness altogether.

Finally, on the fifth day, I took the 7 train to Queens, in search of my first New York address, a building I hadn't been to in the decade since I'd walked out with the same two suitcases I'd come in with. When you emerge from the subway in Jackson Heights onto Roosevelt Avenue, the rhythms of the city alter, spirited away on the strings of a sitar and the gentle slaps of a tabla. There is lamb on kebabs and samosas being sold in half a dozen as if they're dough-nuts. There are women in saris and men speaking in what sounds to the untrained ear like a garbled staccato of *p*'s and *b*'s, some of them wearing turbans and others, Yankees caps. This was my neighbor-hood for nearly all of my inaugural 365 days in NYC.

On this particular Sunday in late July, the sun was hot, but not the kind of heat that bubbles off the pavement. The cross breeze between the rows of brick was pleasant and swayed the trees. People who have ever called New York City home would consider it a damn-near perfect day, and having been pelted by the rain and having sloshed through the snow, I would not nitpick at their hyperbole: low humidity, clear sky, smoke billowing from shimmering metal food trucks, the stench of trash gone until the next pickup, allowing the char of exotic meats to permeate the air and pool saliva on your tongue. I bought a kebab, morsels of juicy lamb stacked one atop another. I paused in front of a window displaying white mannequins in brightly colored saris. I shut my eyes and did my best to separate the syllables of the men peddling whatever it is they peddle, their words fading in and out of my native language, as if they were wind chimes that hadn't been properly tuned.

I meandered beyond the bazaar, where the blocks and parallel streets spread like capillaries from the pulsating subway tracks. In the nooks and crannies, there are other ethnicities and quieter cafes. I craved one last bagel and one last cup of coffee. I entered a deli with a quaint seating area and had a plain with heavy schmear, surrounded by women I assume were from Southeast Asia, sipping hot tea and speaking swiftly, a swirl that I could not decipher but was comforted by. For all I knew, they could have been talking about the weather or about old men, same as the Randy Travis song. I slurped my paper cup empty and crumpled the parchment paper dotted with cream cheese, which had oozed from the sides of my bagel. I tossed them in the trash can then continued my hunt, considering the nearly impossible notion that I might bump into the woman or the man I'd once lived with, or that I might possibly catch a glimpse of the young man who'd lived with them, as if there were actually a version of me still roaming the avenues of Queens.

But none of us were there, nor was the apartment building. I recognized a concrete court (what passes for a park in Queens), although it was half the size of what I remembered, the basketball goals where I used to play with neighborhood kids now gone. Maybe I was over one block too many, or maybe the building was there and I just couldn't locate it in the files of my memory, a fuzzy photograph never fully developed. Nothing resonated, and I realized that I hadn't ever taken a true accounting of the exterior of my first New York City home, how many floors it had or what type of handle or knob I'd grasped to open the entryway. Those details did not matter to a twenty-two-year old who couldn't have fathomed that his thirty-two-year-old self would pass him on the street a decade later, retracing the contours of his life.

That's the beauty in and the sadness of nostalgia: It's a longing for a place and a time and people that simply can't exist. But to simply state the definition does not do justice to the feeling, and that was the impetus for this trip, even if I couldn't consciously explain the initial impulse. I had to see for myself, in other words, to find out if New York still had my heart.

It appeared that a public school had been built where the apartment building once stood. The block stirred in me déjà vu, as though my body's internal GPS had stored the number of steps from the subway, even if my eyes couldn't register the landmarks. My instinct said it was the spot, and that spot was, perhaps appropriately, lost to history.

I strolled back toward Roosevelt Avenue to catch a shuttle to LaGuardia. Yet the energy of the city did not propel me as it had before. New York will always be alive with that kinetic pace—emanating from tourists gawking up at the Empire State Building and from people wearing business suits and pant suits on the subway, frantically pecking on their phones, and in young men and women scurrying toward the 7 train, in a hurry to get to that island of many hills to climb. Instead of joining in, I slowly inhaled and exhaled the air of my former neighborhood, regretting that I hadn't appreciated Jackson Heights for its culture, and for its relative calm, assuming then that the constant hum across the East River was where my worth was waiting to be found.

I lingered and took a few pictures. People sidestepped me, some of them huffing, some of them not glancing up from their phones, some of them with the worry of Monday on their minds, the worry of their worth in this city and where it lies. And that too is the beauty of and sadness in nostalgia: I could not have convinced those people to pause and to appreciate this street and the trees that line it, or prove to them that this time and this place and these people will pass them, just as they passed me, forever out of reach.

I am back in Knoxville, writing this final paragraph in a coffee shop, the house I was renting now empty, filled less with memories than with the thoughts of a man yet again just passing through. Last night, after a Lyft dropped me off from the airport, I sat on the empty hardwood floor with my laptop open and waited for the sun to rise. I searched synonyms for *regret* and found *nostalgia*. But when I searched synonyms for *nostalgia*, I did not find *regret*. ◆

Man in the (Rearview) Mirror

PART 2

After sixteen months as an Uber and Lyft driver in Connecticut and Tennessee, I've put 2,838 trips in the proverbial rearview mirror. I'd hoped to reach three thousand rides before I left for Atlanta, but I've learned that living life in milestones can become an addictive, if not dangerous habit, this penchant for justifying days with a belief that they'll eventually matter, rather than believing each one matters regardless of what it might add up to.

I'm here now in the Peach State, sitting in a hotel room across the street from the Braves' old stadium and the long-extinguished torch cauldron from the 1996 Olympics. I can't move into my apartment until tomorrow afternoon, and my furniture won't arrive for another two days. But in the morning I will begin my first day of graduate student orientation at Georgia State University, then teaching orientation the day after that, and then tutoring orientation after that.

Man in the (Rearview) Mirror

It's a sleepy Sunday afternoon, stick-to-your-back humidity, the kind of day when you'd just as soon relax in the A/C and hum about not having a care in the world, and wish it were true. The scene from my eleventh-floor window is desolate, save for the rush of cars and pickups and semis pedal to the metal along the crisscrossing interstate overpasses. The old Braves stadium rests like a retiree, and the vast stretch of bare blacktop yawns with relief. On the other side of the street, directly outside my window, there is a plot of grass dotted brown with dead spots, likely once a thriving greenspace manicured for the hundreds of thousands of Olympic spectators who descended on Atlanta, spectators who probably paid hundreds of dollars a night to stay in this very room. Paved walkways seem to have cut through the small park, and a concrete plot appears to have rested in its center, but all the cement has mostly given way to dry grass or been reduced to gravel. A tow truck is idling in the middle of the corrosion, its front end aimed at Mercedes-Benz Stadium, the gleaming new home of the Falcons in the distance, towering above those busy interstates. My undergrad alma mater, the Tennessee Volunteers, will open their 2017 football season in that dome on Labor Day, eventually winning in double overtime against the Georgia Tech Yellow Jackets, who happen to share my high school's mascot.

I booked this room through a third-party site and didn't know exactly where I'd be located before I clicked the button. So I guess I shouldn't dismiss the coincidences. Like the fact that a leg of the '96 Olympic torch's route ran through my hometown of Kingston, Tennessee. I can still remember, as an eleven-year-old, my late father pushing through the crowds that lined our blocked-off two-lane highway, snapping black-and-white photos for a short newspaper

192

article about the locals who carried the flame. I tend to not find much meaning in coincidences, mostly because you can always find them, if you're in the mood to look. But I can't ignore that this road I'm on has led me to this hotel room in Atlanta on the verge of a third degree and a new career, the coincidence that my father was born in Georgia in 1926 and that he spent the first fourteen years of his life in Fairmount, a one-exit town that I passed on my way here, the same exit you can take to get to Rome.

As a child, I made a few trips from Kingston to Fairmount with my father and mother, but the only visit I can truly recall was when I was fifteen and had just received my learner's permit, less than a year before my father's sudden death. Unbeknownst to my mother, my father let me drive the whole three hours south to see his older sister, a widow in her eighties who took us to eat BLTs at a drug store that still had a soda fountain. We ate pecan pie at her apartment afterward. They drank coffee and I had sweet tea while they discussed bygone years, tossing around the names of siblings and parents and grandparents long passed. I could sense in the commiserating nods that these were memories they had suppressed—a bespectacled, silver-haired brother and a bespectacled, white-haired sister, nearing the ends of their final chapters.

My father was one of seven, maybe eight, I'm not even certain. They're all dead, he and his siblings, and I was only able to meet two of them: my aunt in Fairmount and an uncle who'd enlisted in the army near the end of World War II but never returned from the U.K. I shook the man's hand once, the week he flew to the States for my father's funeral. I never saw him again. The souls of my father's former life don't haunt me, but I believe they kept my father up nights in his last years. I believe I have some trips to make to Fairmount, some walking around to do, maybe face the demons my father never got around to, somewhere off that road that also, coincidentally, leads to Rome.

When I quit my position as senior editor at *ESPN The Magazine* sixteen months ago, after seven years of climbing the corporate ladder, a colleague and friend gave me E. B. White's *One Man's Meat* as a going-away gift. As I mentioned in the preface, it's a collection of essays written by White after he exited New York City and his job at *The New Yorker* and moved with his wife and son to a farmhouse in Maine. "Once in everyone's life there is apt to be a period when he is fully awake," White says in his own preface, "instead of half asleep."

I'm no E. B. White, to be certain, nor did I have a position at ESPN as prestigious as White's was at *The New Yorker*. Nor did I have a family to uproot and relocate from Bristol, Connecticut, to Knoxville, Tennessee, much less a partner to convince that my nice paycheck was coming at a price too great for me to bear. Yet I do know what it is to be fully awake, the first and thus far only time in my life when I've been able to look back on that disenchanted young man as if he is simply a character I've been writing about in a book.

Perhaps that is the ultimate blessing and the ultimate curse of being a writer—to see past the performance of everyday living, yet still have to find a way to live; to become keenly aware of what is propelling you through the moments, and to comprehend that each moment's passing is a thing to be accounted for, for it cannot be lived again. But we, as writers, are human too, and the enormity of our own condition also overwhelms us, occasionally to the extent that we too have no words other than the ones that cannot do justice to the moment.

It is in these moments—like this one in a hotel room in Atlanta, about to embark on a PhD—when I reach for the tangible: the mini-cooler on the desk next to me, filled with my mother's mustard-and-celery-seed coleslaw, and my grandmother's potato salad laced with chunks of her homemade pickles, and the catfish my grandfather caught and then cleaned and then dredged in cornmeal before dunking it in sizzling oil. Inside this cooler are the leftovers from my farewell dinner on a front porch in Tennessee, overlooking a lake called Watts Bar, in a place the locals call Midway, ostensibly named for its purgatory between the counties Roane and Meigs. My grandmother put the coleslaw in a plastic container that once held sour cream and the potato salad in a plastic container that once held whipped cream, a thrifty woman's Tupperware. The catfish (or what remains after I snuck a few pieces on the drive down) is in a Ziploc baggie, the grease potent enough to soften the edges of the plastic.

My half-brother—who is twice my age and who also earned a degree in journalism—has told me he's proud of my writing and what I've accomplished. But he worries that I'll be pigeonholed as a "Southern author" if I keep on writing about potato salad and coleslaw and fried catfish. That's assuming I ever reach an echelon where anyone bothers to saddle me with an aesthetic. I tell him not to worry, though. I tell him if I keep using words like *echelon* and *aesthetic*, then it'll be *alright*. It'll be just fine, I say.

What I haven't said to my mother or to my grandmother or to my grandfather is that inside this mini-cooler is my favorite meal, a meal that I could probably have most any weekend when the catfish are biting. That is, if I'd stick around for a while, if I didn't have this pang of guilt for growing complacent, for being given a voice and a perspective that I fear will turn stale if I stay on that lake, surrounded by the people who put their love into the food inside these heartbreakingly modest containers.

Where I'm from, that is a conflicting thing to admit, that the containers we are born into can define us but also limit our perspectives, that the outside world can judge us based on how we speak and what we cook and who we believe in, yet we begin to conform to their judgments, and then we begin to judge the outside world just the same. It is a conflicting and nearly condescending thing to admit that I write for the people where I am from, to prove to the outside world that a container does not define me or them, nor do words like *echelon* and *aesthetic* mean anything other than I've bothered to open a dictionary and read a few books.

Yet, as much as I write for them, I also write to them, the people where I'm from and the person I used to be, having put miles and miles between me and that lake most all of my adult life—in places like Queens, New York, and Hartford, Connecticut, and now in Atlanta, places where people tell me I ought not go because of the traffic, where you damn sure don't walk around after dark, places where I ought to maybe think about buying a gun if I'm going to keep letting strangers in my car.

This isn't the final thing I plan to write about my life as an Uber and Lyft driver. But it does feel like the end of a chapter—sixteen months and 2,838 trips I'll always look back on in that idyllic tone, in that way of never being able to view the world with precisely the same set of wide-open eyes. By the time you read this, I will have accepted some government aid and signed a teaching contract for a few thousand dollars above the Federal Poverty Level for a single individual. I will have done it in the name of convincing college freshmen that their words can impact the world. I will have done it in the name of convincing myself that the same applies to me.

I will also have traded my Tennessee license plate for one with black numbers and letters against a stark white background, a Georgia peach hiding there in plain sight. I will have driven Uber Pool and Lyft Shared, allowing passengers to split the fare with other riders going in the same direction, rendering the people in my backseat as foreign to one another as they are to me. Uber now even allows people to send me to pick up packages and to-go orders, rating me on my skills as a delivery boy. But Uber and Lyft will inevitably morph into my side gigs, something to do between writing papers and grading them. By the time you read this, I will have mostly disappeared again into the formalities of society's structure, into alarm clocks and due dates and office hours spent in a cubicle.

Which is perhaps why I'm most nostalgic for these past sixteen months, a period when Uber and Lyft were as much my social life as a paycheck. I drove people around in the morning and in the middle of the day and well after dark. I bore witness to life's ebb and flow, the tangible parts of our day-to-day that we often aren't privy to inside a cubicle or behind a desk or on our couches, staring at smartphones or laptops or flat screens. I counseled passengers nervous about new jobs and leaving old ones. I commiserated with riders ending relationships and en route to first dates. I discussed life's minutiae as if the trivial were as valuable as a twenty-dollar tip.

As is often the case when this blank page overwhelms me, I'm sitting in a coffee shop located on the bottom floor of a downtown Atlanta high-rise that used to belong to a bank. Now the building houses some of Georgia State's academic departments. My cubicle is on the twenty-second floor, although only one student has visited me thus far. I'm also settled into my one-bedroom apartment east of the city, that night in the hotel room seeming like a lifetime ago instead of just three weeks. I've been told teaching can do that to a person, cause the calendar to flip while the world around you seems to be standing still.

It's a sunny Friday morning, and the Braves play the Miami Marlins tonight. There's a beer festival going on too, in a gentrifying neighborhood near downtown. The evening should be profitable behind the wheel. Plus, Hurricane Irma is bearing down on the Southeast coastline, bringing hundreds of thousands of evacuees north. Relaxing in this coffee shop, sun spilling in through four glass walls, my thoughts are on those people already displaced and who could be for a while. My thoughts are on those in Texas, a daunting recovery from Harvey ahead.

My thoughts are on some definitive lesson after these past sixteen months, what a person gains from driving around nearly three thousand strangers. A quote by the late author and educator E. L. Doctorow is up on my laptop screen: "Writing is like driving at night in the fog. You can only see as far as your headlights, but you can make the whole trip that way." I'm not much on inspirational quotes or devotionals, same as coincidences, but I return to this line during almost every essay or story I write. And for whatever reason, coffee shops clear the fog a bit for me, remind me that people do laugh and don't spend their days drinking coffee and staring at walls alone, that the world is not as dark as it can seem to be while I'm traveling this road.

But through the carefree conversations and sunshine, all I can see through the fog on this Friday morning is a white woman and her son, two people who got in my car on a cold February night six months ago. I picked them up at Walmart, and the mother and son filled my trunk with groceries. She'd cashed her first paycheck since starting behind the register at a truck stop and travel center. Mom sat in the back, the boy up front. "He'll get sick on them curvy roads," she said, although I hadn't asked for an explanation. They'd only been in Knoxville a couple of weeks, having left behind Charleston, South Carolina, for reasons that were never revealed to me. She said they were living with her brother until she could put a few more checks in the bank. The woman told me her brother had been kind enough to let them stay on his couch, that her and her son were sleeping in shifts, him during the day while she worked, her at night.

"I gotta get that boy in school, though," she said.

The boy didn't speak. He stared out the windshield, clutching a Nerf gun that his mother had bought him in Walmart. He wore glasses and an indifferent expression. He was dark-headed, like his mother, neither of them dressed in particularly distinguishable manners—jeans and T-shirts and thin jackets and what we call tennis shoes in the South, even though not many of us take up tennis. He seemed older than the Nerf gun implied, maybe thirteen or fourteen. Something in the way he occasionally shifted in his seat as his mother told their story, as though he comprehended the gravity of their situation in a way his mother couldn't, or couldn't afford to, lest she become overwhelmed with all that was on her shoulders.

They were obviously down on their luck, so I was careful not to pry or ask any questions that might be inconsiderate. We could speculate as to why, you and I, same as passing a person huddled into a ball on the street or panhandling along the side of an interstate exit ramp. We could speculate about whether the mother deserved a break, or deserved affordable health care, or deserved redistribution of wealth. Some might say at least she was behind a register. Some might even admire her more if I told you that she walked those curvy backroads to the truck stop, that this Lyft ride was courtesy of her brother's account. But we could also judge the woman for putting her son in this predicament, sleepless nights and a stunted education. We could do a lot of things from where we sit.

I tried to engage the boy by asking what his interests were, how he stayed busy all night while his mother slept. But she chimed in: "He plays them games on my phone," she said. "I can barely keep up with all the data that boy needs." The boy just wore his same expression and clutched his Nerf gun.

"I sure am hungry," the woman said. "You hungry?" she asked the boy. "Too late for anything open," she said without letting her son answer.

"Always Taco Bell," I said.

"Now that sounds awful good," she said. "I ain't had nothin' all day, and we can't bust in my brother's bangin' around in the kitchen. His wife's gotta get up early. Hell, it's already near midnight."

"I can take you," I said.

"Awww, never mind," she said. "Sweet of ya, but I'm runnin' up my brother's bill anyhow. And him already put out with us on his couch."

"I'll turn the meter off," I said.

"Would you do that?" the woman said. "I'll get ya something off that dollar menu. A couple of those cheesy roll-ups or whatever."

I went through the empty Taco Bell drive-thru, and the woman announced the order through the back window. The boy nodded at a chicken quesadilla being all right. His mother ordered two for him and two for her, and two cheesy roll-ups for me, despite my insistence that I wasn't hungry. Both of them ripped open the wrappers immediately and began eating. She'd left the window down, and the smell of grease and burnt cheese swirled in the car. I'm usually annoyed by the smacking of lips and swallowing, people chewing with their mouths open, a hyper-awareness of mine. But I didn't mind this. I was glad to hear their hunger subside. The mother didn't say another word, and I wondered if the boy perhaps was mute, if I had insulted him by asking questions he couldn't answer.

When we reached the address, the mother directed me toward a dirt path, which was muddy from an earlier rain shower. It snaked around a one-story house that was visible from the road to a double-wide situated at the bottom of an embankment. A front-porch light was on, a metal folding chair out front, along with a couple of feral cats that scurried for cover upon hearing my engine.

We all three opened our doors, and I popped the trunk. We began unloading the groceries onto the concrete slab where the metal chair rested. The plastic bags were stuffed full of frozen dinners and snack cakes and potato chips. There were cases of Mellow Yellow and Dr Pepper and Coke. The mother had bought an air mattress.

"Can't blow that up tonight," she said. "Wake the whole damn house up."

A man busted through the screen front door. He was dark-headed too, with a scraggly black beard, in dirt-stained blue jeans and boots and a red-and-black-checkered flannel coat, like I imagine lumberjacks wear in winter. He was on crutches, although he seemed to maneuver the cinder block steps rather well.

"Why the hell did you bring him all the way down here?" he growled, half-hobbling. "You know damn well he's gonna get stuck,

Sheila, wake up my damn landlord."

"I can get out," I said. "No problem. I'm a professional." The man didn't bite at my joke or acknowledge me.

"Sorry, Mikey," Sheila said. "We couldn't cart the groceries from up that hill nohow."

"I'm 'bout over this shit," he said. A woman yelled something indiscernible from inside the trailer. "Hell, you done gone and woke her up too." Mikey crutched his way up the cinder block steps and surveyed the scene, the boy and I now a tandem, unloading groceries as if we were soldiers before a drill sergeant.

"I get back out here, this mess better be inside and put up," Mikey said and slammed the screen behind him.

I hustled for the last couple of cartons of Dr Pepper. The boy and I reached for them, touching hands. "I got 'em," he said. "Better get on." I jerked away. He didn't glance up, just stuck his fingers into the creases in the cartons and hoisted them out.

"Sure do appreciate you," Shelia said. She patted her son on the back, and they began the assembly line up the cinder block steps. I shut the trunk and waved good-bye, but they were too busy to return the gesture. I got in and reversed enough to position my car for an angled shot up the embankment, determined not to spin out or backslide.

I looked in the rearview mirror and saw Mikey's disheveled head emerge, barking orders as Shelia and her son carried in the groceries. He had the Nerf gun in his hand, waving it as though the boy might now have to accomplish some act of menial labor to earn it back. I wanted to reverse back down that muddy path and ask the mother and son if they'd like to go with me, just load up everything and we'd figure out something. My grandmother could cook for them, a real meal, and we could send them home with leftovers. I had a foldout couch. I had some books the boy might want to read. I could even teach him how, if he didn't already know.

I had enough fight in me then to conquer whatever burdens they came with. I had enough fight in me then to save them, even though people who know such things tell me I can't save them all. I stared in the rearview mirror, and I wondered what I will always wonder: Why them and not me? ◆

EPILOGUE

The Price
of Admission

I can't afford to regret. . . . I have to live in the present. The life back
then is gone just as surely—it's as remote to me as if it had happened to somebody I read about in a nineteenth-century novel. I
don't spend more than five minutes a month in the past. The past
really is a foreign country, and they do things differently there.

—RAYMOND CARVER, as quoted in the *Paris Review*'s
"The Art of Fiction," 1983

It's a warm morning in April 2017, a few days shy of my thirty-sec-
ond birthday. I have on a navy sport coat and a loosened green-and-
navy tie. I watched my grandfather, my mother's father, be lowered
into the ground today. But there was no post-funeral gathering, no
celebration of life, at least not one that I was invited to.

   I am writing this from a Starbucks inside a Kroger grocery store
near my hometown of Kingston, Tennessee. My mother is not here,
and she was not there. Perhaps I'm writing this because I believe

she is owed something, although I also believe that I owe the man in the ground something. My grandmother divorced him before I was born, and I grew up visiting her and her second husband far more often. I still endearingly refer to her now-second ex-husband as "Granddaddy." He is the man called "grandfather" in these essays, and, in fact, Granddaddy was there today beside me to pay respects to a man who had never shown him any. I had not spoken to the man who was laid to rest—"Papaw," I called him—in two or three years, not until I went to see him before Parkinson's finally got the better of him at eighty-five years old.

He was cooped up in the same room he'd been resigned to for the last three years, at an assisted-living facility overlooking the Clinch River in Kingston. I doubt it was the place he would've chosen to die, considering my grandmother—the mother of his two daughters, the woman he'd crawl back to every time a girlfriend lost her luster, until she wouldn't have him back anymore—lives happily and healthily less than ten miles down the river. But sometimes the end isn't up to us.

Papaw had been battling what was diagnosed as Parkinson's for about two decades and had become not fully "at himself." Or so my grandmother would tell me when delivering the second-hand news on my visits home from Connecticut. I was still working for ESPN then and had received word that my mother and my aunt, her younger sister, had quit speaking over the care and guardianship of their father, and that my mother had sworn not to visit him again. Having no genuine affinity for the man, I stopped visiting too, a half-hearted show of support for my mother, but mostly an excuse to make one less visit while home on vacation and holidays. Even after my official return to Tennessee, I hadn't bothered to reconnect.

So when my uncle gave me the courtesy of a death bed phone call, I remained conflicted. A visit would go against my new maxims of not living life out of obligation and of not lying to myself and others about my genuine feelings. I knew my aunt would be hovering over the man, and I would not muster the courage to say what was on my mind; nor would I be able to ask him the honest questions—about his infidelities toward my grandmother and his seeming lack of love for my mother, his own daughter.

I did visit that pitiful room, though, in part to stave off any guilt that might've plagued me had I not gone. But there was also a morbid sense of curiosity, to see a man's life made tangible, something I had not seen in more than sixteen years, not since my own father died. I wondered if the distance would somehow render the sight of death more impactful or less, just a fact of life that doesn't worry me much anymore, mostly because I've never let myself get close enough to anyone to miss them when they're gone.

My aunt was there, seated in a rocker right next to his motorized bed, patting his hand and repeating, "Daddy, LaRue's here." My uncle sat in a straight-back chair on the other side of the room, removed from the scene, and I stood wedged between the man's bed and the wall, the light from the window behind me billowing into the room. "Hey, Papaw," was all I could muster. His eyes would open occasionally when my aunt spoke, but they weren't focused on anything, not in this world at least. Toward the end of Parkinson's, a person doesn't shake anymore, more or less catatonic. He wore bifocals, and his receding hair and full beard were trimmed. The beard had been white as long as I'd been alive. He was Santa's doppelgänger when he grinned. Same potbelly, same rosy cheeks, his eyes nearly lost inside his head when he laughed. My mother laughs like that; so do I, the crow's feet about the only thing that gives away my age. But the jovial smile, which had always belied his lukewarm heart, was gone now, his mouth drawn into a constant pucker, having to suck water from a tiny sponge.

I doubt he knew who I was, or even knew I was in the room, although I'm not certain he would've cared. My grandfather never did anything to me and never did much for me, other than put a twenty-dollar bill in a card on holidays and birthdays. There are pictures that prove otherwise, but I only remember him stepping foot in the house I grew up in on the day I graduated high school. At some point before I was born, he'd finally met a woman who corralled him into marriage again, the woman I knew as "Mamaw," and the two of them stayed near the door while everyone congregated throughout our one-story home, packed into the kitchen and dining room, eating and drinking and congratulating me. My grandmother was there, and I imagine that might've been what kept him near the door, afraid to glimpse his old life, what could've been. Papaw and Mamaw were there ten or fifteen minutes, enough time to hand me a card with twenty dollars in it.

Seeing the man now, shriveled and helpless, I considered his palpable discomfort in crowds. Having lived a little myself, I suspect his social awkwardness had something to do with the sense that people were judging him, a guilty conscious about his choices. I've felt the same watchful eyes on me, the irrational fear that every person I encounter can find the faults in my eyes. And maybe there's something to be admired in that, a man having a conscious, no matter how selfish his need for absolution might be.

After my obligatory ten or fifteen minutes were up, I said, "Love ya, Papaw," and then slid out from behind the bed and out the door.

The last words I said to him were worth as much as those twenty-dollar bills I'd received in cards all those years, and I feel guiltier now about going to see him alive than if I hadn't gone at all.

There isn't anything more complicated than a bunch of people forced together for no other reason than blood, people expected to love and respect one another when, as my grandmother would say, Lord knows none of us deserves it. I drove an hour this morning to be beside those people at my grandfather's burial. I woke up before dawn and tied a single Windsor, like my father had taught me, so I could make the trip from Knoxville to a place you can blink and miss, just another of the nondescript towns cut into the hillsides of the East Tennessee Valley. Wartburg's full of hardworking, predominantly God-fearing Germans, my heritage on my grandfather's side. Many of them are Lutherans too, the faith I was raised in. Wartburg was where my grandfather grew up, and where he ultimately settled after he'd married Mamaw, who'd passed away while I was still living in the Northeast, although I didn't come home for her funeral. I hadn't been to the town in probably seven years.

The sky was overcast and a mist floated above the treetops along the two-lane highway. An old gas station occasionally appeared on either shoulder, the pumps out front the kind with numbers that shuffle like a slot machine. They hadn't been filled with gasoline for a while, not enough traffic to continue selling anything but cigarettes and beer, maybe a Little Debbie cake and a Co-Cola. There are secrets in those stations and in the hillsides that cradle them. They are the secrets of my grandfather. They are not mine, but I've heard them whispered more and more as the years have piled up. And while I can't verify their validity, my grandmother hasn't told me a lie in her life. If there is anything I can take to the grave, it is that.

My grandmother will be nearly eighty-five by the time you read this, and she has entered that stage when the stories become a memory playlist on shuffle. She tells me often of my grandfather's work with an electrical company that was stringing telephone lines across the United States during the '50s and '60s, stringing their young family from trailer park to trailer park. My mother attended school in five different states before the fifth grade. Once, somewhere around Wisconsin, my grandmother says that her husband convinced her to put herself and her two tiny daughters on a bus back to Tennessee. He claimed he wouldn't be far behind, but he was actually seeing another woman. By the time she reached the bank to take out money for groceries, my grandfather had withdrawn every dime. My grandmother had to borrow from her own father until she could resume her job as a looper at the hosiery mill, the only profession her eighth-grade education afforded her. She took my grandfather back, over and over, worried that she couldn't provide for her daughters on her own, until they were finally old enough to fend for themselves.

There are more stories like that about my grandfather—taking condiments from his family's refrigerator out of spite, the sheets right off the bed—but that one is enough to tell you what kind of man we're dealing with. Winding through the hillsides of Wartburg, I tried to make sense of that story and all the others, trying to determine whether a man deserves to be defined by more than his mistakes, even after he's in the ground. I spent most of the drive wondering who's going to spill all my secrets after I'm gone.

• • •

I always grin at the sign that reads "City Limits" when the pine trees dissolve into a couple of traffic lights and a Sonic and a Hardees and a used-car dealership and Partner's Pizza, which isn't half-bad pizza, if you ever find yourself in Wartburg, Tennessee. Like any small town worth its salt, Wartburg's funeral home is a staple in the city limits, positioned in the middle of town so the respects being paid can be carried on the gossip that spreads from the valley into the hillsides. There'd been a receiving of friends the night before, but I didn't go, not wanting to stand in line and shake hands on behalf of a man I was indifferent about.

I pulled into the parking lot, greeted by familiar cars and pickups that were already single file behind the black hearse, magnetic signs atop each one emblazoned with "FUNERAL." I parked and walked toward the front door but was met by a tall, dark-headed white man with a gold name tag pinned to his suit coat.

"Are you a member of the family?" he asked and extended his hand.

I put my hand into his, firm like us Southern men do, and said, "Yes, sir."

"You'll want to pull round behind the others, unless you're riding," he said.

I didn't know who would be inside the funeral home, but I knew before I ever tied my single Windsor that I'd drive from the funeral home to the cemetery and from the cemetery straight out of Wartburg, likely never setting foot inside the city limits again.

"I'll drive," I said and went back to my car. As I maneuvered into position behind all the others, I saw the man weaving his way through the line with one of those magnetic FUNERAL signs. He slapped it atop my car.

"Your family's inside," he said, "paying their final respects. Sorry for your loss."

"Appreciate it," I said. He shut my door for me, as if I was someone who needed that, someone who needed consoling. I wanted to stand right there with him, wished I could just ignore all the insincerity of what was about to transpire inside that room where the dead man was lying supine, his face powdered and painted, perhaps by this very man standing in front of me. I would have rather discussed what that's like, painting and powdering the faces of dead people, day after day, than talk to the living about memories tainted by my grandmother's stories, and by the absence of my mother, who refused to visit a man in death who hadn't wanted her to visit him in life. The man with the name tag must've recognized my hesitance, because he said, "These days aren't ever easy, Son, but he's with the Lord now."

I nodded and smiled and walked through the double doors, the frame wide enough for a casket flanked by pallbearers to pass through. The mustiness of old wood and carpets shampooed and shampooed over decades enveloped me, along with the smells of suits long tucked away in closets, mingling with thick perfumes and hairsprays that had settled into the plaster walls. My aunt spotted me, gave me a tired smile. She is a thin woman with light eyes and light hair, nothing like my mother, who has dark hair that she dyes and who has always been a few dress sizes bigger than her younger sister. When I was a kid, people would assume I belonged to my aunt and that my cousin was my mother's child. My cousin was there too—tall, thin, and dark-headed, lingering behind her mother. Even as adults, I can't read my cousin, not sure if she's shy or just reserved, able to disappear in any room or family function. She is a year older and already has two adolescent girls of her own, a divorce behind her. I used to be the only family member who could coax her into talking, but the years and miles between us have created a silence of convenience, too much life gone to start over.

I hugged my aunt and shook my uncle's hand and waved to my cousin. Besides the four of us, there were two other extended family members in the room and an elderly woman I didn't recognize. The woman could only stand in spurts and stayed seated in a metal chair, offering stories to anyone who was close enough to listen, about people she figured we all knew, who lived in the hillsides of Wartburg, people who had once known my grandfather as a young man. The two men with gold name tags pinned to their coats looked on, expressionless.

My cousin and I receded to the edges of the room, like we were back at the kids table during Thanksgiving and Christmas. She'd left her girls in school.

"Is your mom coming?" she asked.

"She's not," I said.

Her eyes watered up. She seemed to be asking, "Will everything be different?"

Our family, our Thanksgivings and our Christmases, birthdays and reunions at the lake where my grandmother lives. It would change everything, already had. I knew that as well as she did, and I felt sorry for my cousin then because, unlike me, she had held on to a notion of a thing that I'd lost hope in a long time ago, back when I watched my own father be lowered into the ground. Maybe having children of her own had caused her to wish for a sense of family that was fading.

She avoided my silence with another question about her half-brother, the product of my aunt's second marriage, asking whether

I'd seen him or heard if he was coming. He'd apparently agreed to be a pallbearer, but there was no sign of him, and the funeral procession was scheduled to begin soon. My aunt had informed me that she'd removed my name from the list of pallbearers a couple of years ago, when I was still living up North. "Just didn't know if we could rely on you," she'd said, "and everything with your mom. I thought you might not want to anymore." I'd smiled, held my tongue, like us Southern men do.

I shrugged to my cousin about her brother and made a promise to myself that I wouldn't lay a hand on those pallbearer rails, if asked. I left my cousin and stood in front of the open casket, a slideshow of photographs displayed on a screen above: the dead man smiling with his daughters and with his grandchildren and with Mamaw. My mother was in a few of them, perhaps a symbolic olive branch from my aunt, who'd selected the pictures. My grandmother wasn't in any of them, though. The dead man in the casket looked the same as I'd seen him the week before, except his cheeks weren't rosy and his eyes weren't open. My father's casket was closed because half his head had been shaved prior to the brain surgery that stopped the hemorrhaging from his fall. My mother didn't want him to be exposed that way, without him there to say how he wanted to be remembered. But they allowed the immediate family to see him before the burial, and some nights that lifeless face is in my dream, half bald-headed, the last image I have in my mind of my father. I'd become my own man in the sixteen-plus years since his death. But I still have that teenager inside of me, that fifteen-year-old boy who sure would like someone to stand beside him in times like these, when you realize that everything has changed, that you're alone even in a room full of family.

I strained for guilt, for never putting forth any effort to create a bond with my Papaw in life. But all the pain he'd caused our family was too suppressed to unearth in death, a wound so deep for my mother that what life she has left isn't enough for it to become a scar. I turned and scanned the funeral home, which had acquired more bodies belonging to the family of Mamaw, the dead man's daughter-in-law and two grandsons by marriage, whom I hadn't seen since we were kids. They had entered my grandfather's life in his later years, as a calmer, more agreeable man. I don't believe these people recognized me as an adult, my glasses and my facial hair and the thin frame I've developed from years of running, literally and figuratively. They glanced at me with recognition but moved on to the faces they were certain of, my aunt and uncle and cousin, who'd remained in contact with them.

"Please say your final respects and head to your cars," one of the men with the gold name tags announced. "The procession will begin shortly."

I watched all the men assume their positions as pallbearers, although my cousin, my aunt's son, was nowhere to be found. One of the men with the gold name tags pinned to his coat took my cousin's spot at the casket. I lagged behind the women, alongside the man I call Granddaddy, who'd arrived quietly, there in support of my aunt, his former daughter-in-law, even though he wasn't a part of this mess, not by blood or by marriage. I shook his hand, a shared understanding between us that we didn't belong any more than the man with the gold name tag did, carrying a casket containing a dead man neither of us ever really knew.

• • •

Epilogue: The Price of Admission

I'd forgotten what it's like to experience the unspoken Southern protocol of a funeral procession: the cars and pickups of strangers pulled to the sides of the road out of respect as we passed, the idea being that every person deserves at least that.

The procession snaked around the few markers of modern society in Wartburg, the fast-food restaurants and a chain grocery store, until we reached the town square, with a tiny post office and a historic courthouse, Wartburg being the seat of Morgan County. Then the two-lane highway became lined on either side with fields of high grass and double-wide trailers and one-story ranchers, and then the cemetery, the gray cement of the headstones stretching into the pale blue of the horizon.

We obediently parked in another straight line along a gravel drive and took our places around a green tent that had been set up at the corner of the cemetery nearest the main road. Underneath the tent was a short row of chairs and beneath them a mat of cheap, fake turf meant to conceal that we were all gathered at a hole in the ground. I stayed to the back of the group and avoided eye contact, lest my aunt or uncle wave me over to sit under the tent. The pallbearers positioned the casket above the abyss, and the preacher, in his clerical collar, took his position by its side. My aunt and my uncle and my cousin sat under the tent while I stood outside, no one behind me, Granddaddy next to me.

The preacher began his eulogy, and I bowed my head in the right places and said "Amen" in the right places but did not shut my eyes. The serenity of the scene was pierced by a beat-up truck buzzing by, the ear-splitting roar of an engine's pistons firing without a muffler. The shrill sound soothed me—the lack of reverence, the whoop and holler from the truck's open windows, men drunk before noon on

215

a weekday, getting through the monotony the best they know how. The preacher raised his voice, doing his best to ignore the fact that the pomp and circumstance of a funeral didn't block out the world's sin. Then he launched into a Lutheran tradition, the Apostle's Creed, which I had once been able to recite by heart. The Bible Belt remains cinched around my waist, probably always will be, although I have felt it loosening notch by notch ever since I left Kingston for New York City at twenty-two years old.

It occurred to me, as the preacher recited *From thence He will come to judge the living and the dead,* that I would have to bow and "Amen" through this routine for my grandmother and for my mother, assuming I outlive them. I wasn't quite sure how to stop living life out of obligation, to completely extricate myself from this learned behavior. The preacher lifted his stiff-fingered right hand and outlined a cross in the air, and my grandfather was officially dead.

I shut my eyes, not to pray or to say "Amen," but to hold this image in my mind, barely more than two handfuls of people milling about, the only proof that a man had once walked this earth. My father was gone, and his parents, my other set of grandparents, had been dead decades before I was even born. Counting my half-brother and half-sister, my immediate family was now down to four. I opened my eyes to Granddaddy's soft smile saying, "See you soon enough." I followed the backs of heads as they floated to their cars. I was stopped by my aunt, who said, "Thanks for coming," as if she had understood, all the way back to the assisted-living facility, that I was going through the motions. Maybe she was thanking me because she assumed I was doing it for her. I wasn't. I was doing it partly for my grandmother, partly for my mother, but mostly for myself, to comprehend what the end can become, how lonely and desolate it can be for a man who walls himself off from his past and from his sins—an existence as lonely as those gray cement headstones.

My car was the only one without the engine running, the line patiently waiting to be released. Each vehicle had been relieved of its FUNERAL sign. I climbed in and turned the key. I let out a slow breath, the same sensation I had as a teenager after suffering through two hours on a hardwood pew every Sunday morning. I was reminded of how living life out of obligation can become what sustains you, what keeps you confined to a small town surrounded by people who love you simply because of the blood you share. I never told Papaw how much we had in common: how I cheated on my girlfriend of six years, how I've cheated or lied to every woman I've been romantically involved with, how I can't fathom loving a child more than myself, how I began dating a single mother once I was back in Tennessee, and how I already knew I would not be able to commit to her either, a nagging sense that I can never be the man she deserves and certainly not a stepfather to her son. I wasn't ready to tell her that day, didn't yet have the words to explain that the man in the ground and I are all too similar, that I don't believe I can be a devout partner to anyone in this life, much less a husband out of necessity, like I was taught all those Sundays on hardwood pews.

I started this essay in that Kroger near Kingston, Tennessee, a few days shy of thirty-two. I'm thirty-three now, and I thought this time in Atlanta—a fresh start as a single man, a PhD student, and a teacher—would be about learning to love myself again, to be proud of my accomplishments, the man I'm becoming. But I've only begun to question the sincerity of my intentions—how I've treated women, how I've distanced myself emotionally from my family so that I don't have to deal with the pain of all we've never said, all that's been laid to rest without resolution.

In the beginning I led you to believe that the impetus for this journey, my decision to leave ESPN and become an Uber driver, was to face my father's death. The problem is that I'm not sure what the truth is anymore, can't even be certain that I'm aware of my own blind spots. In the process of peeling back the layers, I wonder if I've conveniently lied to myself about what's beneath them, what's been eroding my heart.

When I was twenty years old, a junior at the University of Tennessee, I got blackout drunk and put my hands on a woman, around the neck of the girl I'd been dating since we were sophomores in high school. For thirteen years now, I've been conflicted over whether I owe that information to everyone I meet, to any woman I lie next to in bed. I've told a few of them, but not all of them and certainly not every person I've met, not friends nor family. I put my hands on her again at twenty-one, again alcohol-induced, and I have a scar from eight stiches the time she hit me in the mouth with a cell phone. Had the police been called the first time, I probably would've been arrested, potentially sent to rehab or anger management, maybe even had assault on my record. This book turns out much different, or not at all. But there is no tangible proof, other than the scar on my upper lip, and now these words between two covers.

"Put my hands on a woman" is an innuendo that leaves every-thing to the imagination, like the Southernism "on account of his nerves," which we use to describe a man who ought to visit a doc-tor or a therapist, but we send him to a preacher instead. I might write the shameful details of those events in another essay before I'm in the ground, but my side of the story doesn't seem to matter much, not at this stage in the healing process, other than the fact of admission. I have said, "I'm sorry." We were twenty-three, and I was home from New York City, down about twenty-five pounds from the depression, from the running. We cried and hugged but were too young to comprehend the severity of what I'd done, how those drunken episodes would alter our mental and physical health, change our lives irreversibly into nothing we'd bargained for. I haven't communicated with her in at least five, six years. She did text to say that she hadn't attended our ten-year high school reunion because she'd heard I'd be there.

The rage isn't inside of me anymore, but I can't promise that the guilt is any less dangerous. So I warn women these days, up front, present as honestly as I can the shell of a man they're dealing with. I've had PhD colleagues ask me why students open up to me on such a personal level, and while I don't confess every sin to my students, I do read to them about the death of my father, about my emotional unavailability and infidelity, about my abuse of alcohol to the point of arrest. I confide in them because I believe they can find solace in writing, that they have the opportunity to heal and to potentially avoid my mistakes. I urge them to visit the free counseling center on campus, tell them that therapy is nothing to be ashamed of, that they shouldn't wait more than a decade like I did.

People open up to me, whether during my office hours or in my Honda Civic, because they sense that I won't judge them. That's all people really want—to be accepted and to be forgiven, to offer the worst of themselves and not be reduced to a "cheater" or a "liar" or a "wife beater" or an "alcoholic." Not until I watched a man I'd unfairly judged be lowered into the ground did I realize that I was headed for the same fate, a man buried with his sins. People

I've confided in say that I have to forgive myself. But I haven't. In the quote that opens this essay, Raymond Carver, a writer who's had a profound influence on my prose, says that he "can't afford to regret," alluding to years of alcoholism and crimes committed, including allegedly putting his hands on his first wife. While I admire Carver as a writer of fiction, I disagree with him as a man. All I can afford is regret. And as for not spending "more than five minutes a month in the past," we don't have a choice but to spend every day in our past—because our present doesn't exist without it, nor does our future.

I tell my students that our choices are important, that we can actually choose how we leave this world. But the one choice we don't get to make is how we enter it, who we're born to and the past we inherit. I was born white and something around middle class and with a nine-digit number that grants me the luxury of being an "American." I was born to a fifty-nine-year-old man who chose to start over with a woman thirty years younger, a man who surely knew that odds were he might be gone before I needed him most. I was born to a woman whose father didn't seem to want her, a man who didn't seem to want a family at all, but who was born in an era when a man was raised to believe he had no choice.

I'm not attempting to convince myself or you that our fate is predetermined by bloodlines. But there is a harsh reality to be confronted, if we're willing. Which is that the adults in our life pass on their coping mechanisms, and they pass on their belief systems and their judgments. Then one day we're faced with decisions that reveal the adults in our lives might have been making the wrong choices. That isn't placing blame, but it is acknowledging the problem, how the cycle remains unbroken because nothing is more difficult than taking a stand against the very people you're supposed to support unconditionally, the very people who were supposed to steer you straight.

I've heard people use the phrase "only God can judge me" when presented with nuanced issues of their own immorality. The jury's still out for me on a higher power, yet the God I was raised to believe in granted forgiveness inherently, before the sin was even committed. The God I was raised to believe in granted us the free will to forgive ourselves and to forgive others, or to not. The catch is that you first have to look in the mirror and face your sins, to admit them. And, of course, it's always easier to condemn or to forgive when your life isn't the one on trial.

My grandmother, God bless her, says that people who've done the things I've done ought to just be shot cause they're not human anyhow. I don't think, if my grandmother lives to read this, that she'll say her grandson ought to be shot. But my grandmother will be disappointed. My grandmother hasn't told me that she forgives my grandfather, although she has told me that wherever he is, she prays he's at peace. I wish I knew, wish I'd asked Papaw if he was afraid, asked him how a man forgives himself.

My father rarely appears in my dreams anymore, those nights when you're sure he'll be there when you wake up. Once in a while, though, I'll get to see him, and it's as if he didn't die, just disappeared, just needed some rest from me and my mother, to find peace with his past. He hugs me, and then I'm aware inside the dream that we don't have any time left. I ask if he forgives me, and he tells me that forgiveness takes time. He smiles then.

"But you still have time, Son," he says. "We still have a little time yet." ◆

221

ACKNOWLEDGMENTS

Thank you to my father, who instilled in me a passion for storytelling and for the written word. I wish you were here. Thank you to my mother, who has loved and supported me through every life choice, for better and for worse, and thank you to Granny and Granddaddy, whose insights injected life into these essays in immeasurable ways.

My sincere thanks also to my brother and sister, and to my extended family, as well as to the Stevenses, the Randolphs, the Leffews, the Alexanders, and all my East Tennessee folks. Thanks to my NYC family, Jenn and Dan; thanks to my friends and former ESPN colleagues, especially Gueorgui, Hallie, Ross, Paul, Eric, JB, and last but not least, Wank and Max, who let me tag along on the adventures. Thanks to my Fairfield MFA family, especially Eugenia Kim, Alan Davis, Baron Wormser, Michael White, and to Andrew for those nights in Naples. Thanks to my Georgia State family, especially my students, who inspire me. And a special thanks to my good friend Bates, whose couch and late-night calls kept me going.

Much appreciation to Woodhall Press for believing in this project, and to my editor, Colin Hosten, for pushing me and these essays to be more. Finally, if you've read it all, then you know there are people I won't name, but to whom I owe a thank-you for being a part of my life—and for sticking by me far longer than I deserved.

ABOUT THE AUTHOR

In a former life, LaRue Cook was a senior editor at *ESPN The Magazine* and ESPN.com. After an Existential Crisis—and turning thirty—he retreated south to pursue his PhD in creative writing at Georgia State University, where he also teaches English composition and fiction writing. This is his first book.

He holds a degree in journalism from the University of Tennessee at Knoxville and an MFA from Fairfield University in Connecticut. His nonfiction has appeared in such publications as *ESPN The Magazine* and *Reader's Digest*, while his fiction has appeared in *Washington Square Review*, *Barely South Review*, and *Noctua Review*, among other places. He currently resides in Decatur, Georgia, just east of Atlanta, where he's working on a collection of short stories. His home will always be Kingston, Tennessee, if only in spirit.

CPSIA information can be obtained
at www.ICGtesting.com
Printed in the USA
LVHW040953250219
608648LV00004B/93/P